Travellers' Tales

FROM THE STORY OF INVERNESS-SHIRE

HISTORY LIFE LONG AGO LORE LEGENDS AND STRANGE SECRETS

LANG SYNE
PUBLISHING

Publisher's Note

Part One of this booklet is reprinted from an account of Inverness-shire's history published over one hundred years ago. The material was last published by Lang Syne in 1979 in the booklet "From Inverness-shire's Story."

Part Two is a selection of stories from "Selected Highland Folktales" gathered orally by R MacDonald Robertson and published by Oliver and Boyd in 1964. We would like to thank their successors, Longman's Publishers, for granting permission to reprint the stories.

Part Three by Francis Thompson is reprinted from "Highland Smugglers, Second Sight and Superstitions" published by Lang Syne in 1980.

Published by Lang Syne Publishers Ltd, Whitecrook Centre, Clydebank in 1991. Printed by Darnley Press Ltd. at the same address.
Copyright Lang Syne Publishers Ltd 1991.
ISBN 185217 179 0

INTRODUCTION

Step back in time for a fascinating journey that spans more than 2000 years in the story of Inverness-shire. Meet the folk who lived here before the dawn of Christianity and learn about their unusual lifestyles and superstitious beliefs. Discover how later generations marvelled at the miracles of St Columba, who had to act quickly when he came face to face with the Loch Ness Monster!

On our travels we see how wooden forts, built for defence, were replaced by great stone castles, designed for aggression. And at the time locals had a clear choice: clear out of the area or stay on and be forced into slavery.

We stop off in the eighteenth century where an English writer gives a graphic account of life and times in Inverness. Most of the murderers and villains had escaped from the town jail and clan plotting was blamed. A tax on ale to pay for a new quay for commercial ships caused uproar. The streets were excessively dirty, the manners and drinking habits of the residents left a lot to be desired, and houses in the suburbs were just turf hovels with a hole in the roof for a chimney.

Strong claret was kept in pails, funerals lasted a month and were very drunken affairs. In one case, the burial of a clan chief's wife, mourners got so drunk they forgot to bring the coffin. The chiefs themselves ruled with a rod of iron and to offend them risked having one's head chopped off or, if you were lucky, being despatched to the West Indies as a slave!

Many families were condemned to live in wretched poverty. When food was short wives bled the cattle, mixed the blood with a little oatmeal, and fried the whole as a sort of cake.

In 1744 Inverness Town Council condemned the new popular drinks, tea and brandy, as threats to the health of the people. We are given a fascinating insight into the morals of our forefathers at that time and their style of dress comes under particular scrutiny.

Then there were the heartrending experiences of the Glen evictions. Profit was put before people as entire families were uprooted and forced to leave Scotland for ever, first to Australia and then America.

In Part Two we glimpse into the strange and secret world of Inverness-shire folktales and legends. The Evil Eye was a hereditary secret spell passed from generation to generation and, who knows, may still be not uncommon even in the closing years of the 20th century. Victims of this withering optical beam were invariably the prettiest and healthiest children in a Highland village, the choicest cow in the byre, or the best pig in the sty.

Along the way we meet strange characters and learn of odd things. The witch who stole whisky .... the dog whose appearance foretells death for anyone called Gillies or Macdonnell .... the phantom bagpipes heard by men of the Cameron Highlanders .... the spectre in the rowan tree that frightened travellers .... clay images used for witchcraft spells .... the warrior who was the most vicious and evil man ever to be born in the Highlands .... the farmland where nothing could grow because it was for the Devil's own use .... and the peculiar business of the phantom barking dogs.

In Part Three Francis Thompson recalls the days of the whisky smugglers and the clever tricks they played to avoid detection. He tells the fascinating story of Inverness-shire's very own seer who was able to predict all sorts of events. And he writes about the many festivals, traditions and taboos that helped mark time through the years for our ancestors.

Part One

Battles and Magic Spells

When the light of history first breaks upon Inverness-shire we find the country now called Scotland divided into four kingdoms. To the south of the line of the Forth and Clyde lay the kingdom of the Britons of Strathclyde, and that of the Saxons of Northumbria; to the north of that line, those of the Scots and the Picts, separated from each other by the mountain-chain called by the old writers Dorsum Britanniae, or Drumalban, the range of hills dividing Argyll and Perthshire. What is now Inverness-shire lay wholly within the kingdom of the Picts. These were the ancient Caledonians, the fierce people of whom we have descriptions from the Roman historians — men of red hair and long limbs, who had no walled cities, and nothing deserving the name of a town; who lived by pasturage and the

Caledonian warriors hunting for food

chase; who painted their bodies with pictures of wild animals; and who could stand for days immersed in the waters of their marshes. Their language was that now known as the Gaelic; and their capital, or the seat of their king, at the dawn of the Christian era, was at the mouth of the river Ness, possibly on the site now occupied by the capital of the Highlands.

The Picts were divided into two sections — the northern and the southern Picts. The former, called by the Irish annalists the Cruithne Tuath or Cruithne of the North, lay to the north, and the latter to the south, of the range of mountains called the Month, which now bears the name of the Grampians. In the northern portion, at least, the Romans effected no settlement. The geographer Ptolemy, in the second century, speaks of the Varar Aestuarium of Beauly Firth in describing the coast, and preserves for us the ancient name of the people, Caledonii, who inhabited the districts of Badenoch, Stratherrrick, Glengarry, Glenmoriston, Glenurquhart, the Aird, Strathnairn, Strath-dearn,and Athole. These Caledonians were undoubtedly Celts, ancestors of the same people who now inhabit the Scottish

The connection between the northern and the southern Picts was at no time, probably, of a very intimate character. The men of the Highlands and those of the Lowlands, though nominally under the same sovereign, had little in common. They were separated geographically by a wild mountain-chain. Their customs were different, and so for a time was their religion; and when in 843 Kenneth Macalpine, a Scot, obtained the kingship over the southern Picts, those north of the Grampians took up a separate position. They formed themselves into a confederacy of their own, and asserted their independence. The new province that emerged from the severance of the north from the south was called the province of Moray, and comprised most, if not all, of what is now Inverness-shire. It was far more extensive than that which afterwards bore the same name, and stretched from the river Spey on the one side and from Loch Lochy on the other, to Caithness. This territory was governed by a sovereign, sometimes called a Maormor, a title peculiar to the Gaelic people, and sometimes Ri Moreb or King of Moray.

This kingdom had a troubled existence. It was placed between two fires. To the north were the Norsemen, who, obtaining foothold in Orkney, had extended themselves over what are now the counties of Caithness and Sutherland. To the south was the growing kingdom of Scotland, ever ambitious of extending its territory. Between the descendants of the vikings and the inhabitants of the southern kingdom the men of Moray had but little peace. The Ri Moreb had from time to time to enter into an alliance with the one power to protect himself against the other. More than once the Norwegians entirely conquered Moray. A mighty Norse warrior, Thorstein the Red, ruled over the province for a year. In the closing years of the ninth century, Sigurd, Earl of Orkney, followed in his train and overran the country, though his sovereignty did not last very long. The Scottish monarchy also made inroads from the south upon Moray, and King Malcolm, son of Donald, King of Alban, endeavoured to annex, but with small success, the northern province. He slew Cellach, its maormor, but the province retained its independence.

The men of Moray were of a stubborn and indomitable character, and they fought both their northern and their southern foes with desperation. They were a fighting race, and when not attacked by their neighbours they made forays upon them. In 1020 Finlaec or Findlay, maormor of Moray, entered Caithness with a large army and challenged the Norse earl, Sigurd, to meet him in battle. The Norwegian, aided by the men of Orkney, accepted the challenge, and the maormor was defeated. Sigurd, pursuing his victorious way southward, overran the provinces north of the Spey, and Moray became again, and remained, it is supposed, for two years, a Norwegian province. On the death of Sigurd it again resumed its independence. In the end the brave little province fell into the hands, not of its northern, but of its southern, neighbour.

How this was brought about, and how Moray became incorporated with Scotland, may here be briefly told. It is not necessary to give details which do not immediately concern our narrative. In 1003 the King of Scotland, King Malcolm, died, leaving two grandsons, Duncan, and Thorfin Earl of Caithness. Between the two the contest for the throne was long and fiercely waged. The maormor of Moray at the time was Macbeth, a name made famous by the great dramatist; and from the position of his territory, lying between the combatants, his alliance was naturally regarded as of the utmost importance by both claimants. At first he sided with King Duncan, and his territory suffered in consequence. Thorfin and his Norsemen were victorious, and Moray was desolated with fire and sword. King Duncan then collected an army and hurried north, and a battle ensued at Burghead, in which the Norsemen were again the victors. They drove the fugitive Scots before them, and conquered the country all the way to Fife. At this stage King Duncan was deserted by the maormor of Moray, who attached himself to Thorfin. He felt that his interests lay rather with his victorious northern neighbour than with the Scots.

The traditional story of his murdering King Duncan is well known, and, as Sir Walter Scott says, has been adopted by Hollinshed, dignified by the classical Latinity of Buchanan, and dramatised by Shakespeare. It is with a sigh of regret that the historian has to regard the picturesque tale as utterly mythical; to remember that no such persons as Banquo and Fleance ever existed, and that the famous scene in the castle of Inverness never took place. All we do know is, that King Duncan was slain in some conflict with Macbeth at a place called Bothgowan near Elgin. The name Bothgowan means a smith's house, where perhaps Duncan sought shelter when the battle went against him, and where he met his fate by the sword of his former ally.

Thorfin, the Norwegian, and Macbeth divided between them, the conquered territory. Thorfin ruled the North, including the province of Moray, which thus again became

Norwegian. Macbeth became king of the southern district beyond the Grampians, which had Scone as its capital, where he ruled as King of Scotland for seventeen years. At the end of that period he was dethroned. Malcolm Caenmore, son of the murdered Duncan, advanced against him from the south, drove him across the Month, and slew him at Lumphanan in Mar. In the year in which Macbeth met his fate, his ally Thorfin died, and Moray became again a kingdom. Malcolm, however, wanted control, and invaded it in 1078. He conquered the hereditary ruler Maelsnectan, who escaped with his life, and who died seven years after in a fortress of Lochaber in which he had taken refuge. Moray thus became a part of Scotland, though the power of the kings over the wild northern territory was for many years more nominal than real, maormors holding sway there oftener than once.

It is pleasant to turn from this troublous story of incessant warfare, which preceded the absorption of Inverness-shire into Scotland — a story which historians have disentangled from the accounts of Irish-analysts, Saxon chronicles, and Norwegian sagas — to tell of the coming of Christianity to our county, and of its peaceful triumphs.

The religion of the northern Picts at the advent of Christianity was entirely pagan, and was apparently the same in kind as that followed by their neighbours the Scots. Holding a high place among both Scots and Picts was a class of men called Druids. They are frequently mentioned in the lives of Columba and Patrick, and in the ancient Celtic manuscripts which have come down to us from Irish sources. They dwelt at the residence of the kings, and exercised great powers in national affairs; but beyond that we know little about them. There are no grounds for asserting that they formed a sacerdotal order. They appear to have been magicians, soothsayers, and enchanters — workers of spells and charms — their influence with the people being founded on the belief that by their "special powers" they could aid those who sought their assistance, or injure those opposed to them. If the Druids were in any sense the ministers of a religion, it was of a debased and grovelling kind, a species of fetichism, an adoration of natural objects and of the powers of the external world, the rocks, the winds, the thunder. Among the pagan Scots, and probably among their neighbours, pillar-stones were objects of worship, and were either overthrown or were consecrated with the sign of the cross by the Christian teachers. The Picts also seem to have believed in what were called the Sidhe — spirits who were supposed to haunt nature and to dwell underground.

St Columba seems to have had full belief in the existence of these demons, which were supposed to have their dwelling-places in fountains and green hillocks. He delighted in exorcising them. "While the blessed man was stopping," says his biographer, "in the province of the Picts, he heard that there was a fountain famous among the heathen people, which foolish men, having their reason blinded by the devil, worshipped as a god. For those who drank of the fountain, or who purposely washed their hands or feet in it, were allowed by God to be struck by demoniacal art, and went home either leprous or purblind, or at least suffering from weakness, or some kind of infirmity.

"By all these things the pagans were seduced, and they paid divine honours to this fountain. Having ascertained this, the saint one day went up to the fountain fearlessly; and on seeing this, the Druids, whom he had often sent away vanquished and confounded, were greatly rejoiced, thinking that, like others, he would suffer from the touch of that baneful water. The saint then blessed the fountain, and from that day the demons departed from the water; and not only was it not allowed to injure anyone, but even many diseases among the people were cured by this same fountain after it had been blessed and washed in by the saint."

A Superstitious People

From such notices as these in the lives of the saint we may form some idea of what was the early pagan religion of Inverness-shire. Some traces of this paganism survive at the present day. In the belief in charms, in fairies, in witchcraft, in the power of the evil eye, which still lingers in Highland glens, we have relics of the old Celtic heathenism still existing in the midst of our present civilisation. Such superstitions were treated very gently by the early Christian teachers, and perhaps on that account have survived. Fountains were blessed and became holy wells. Demonology was recognised, and exorcism practised. The advice given by one of the Popes to British missionaries was, that they should disturb pagan practices as little as was necessary. You cannot, he argues, cut off everything at once from rude natures.

It is possible that St Columba was not the first pioneer of Christianity in Inverness-shire. The mountains that divided Moray from Christian peoples were not impassible by Christian teachers, and one of these, Merchard, from beyond the Month, is known to heve settled in Glenurquhart. He may have been one among others like him. But in that early time St Columba is the outstanding figure in a light almost modern in its clearness. In the year 565 he made a pilgrimage, accompanied by two companions, Congal of Bangor and Kanneach of Achaboe, to the Court of the King of the Picts. His biographer Adamman tells in graphic language of his interview with King Brude at his palace, situated in the neighbourhood of the river Ness.

When the saint arrived at the palace of the king he was refused admittance. "The king, elated by the pride of royalty, acted haughtily, and would not,open his gates to the blessed man. When the man of God observed this, he approached the folding-doors with his companions, and having first formed

The gate flew open instantly at St Columba's command

upon them the sign of the cross of our Lord, he then knocked at and laid his hand upon the gate, which instantly flew open of its own accord, the bolts having been drawn back with great force. The saint and his companions then passed through the gate thus speedily opened, and when the king heard what had occurred, he and his councillors were filled with alarm; and immediately setting out from the palace, he advanced with due respect to meet the blessed man, whom he addressed in the most conciliatory and respectful language, and ever after from that day, as long as he lived, the king held this holy and revered man in very great honour, as was due." The result of the saint's meeting and intercourse with Brude was that the king was baptised, and probably owing to his power over his subjects the work of Columba in preaching the Gospel among them was made a lot easier.

In Adamman's life of Columba we have many notices of the saint's work beyond the dorsal range of Britain, and many of his miracles are recounted as taking place in Inverness-shire. These acccounts are too numerous to give at length. They are all of the same marvellous character. Sometimes in his travels he traversed the great glen of Scotland which leads to Loch Ness, probably striking the glen through the pass which terminates at Laggan, between Loch Oich and Loch Lochy; sometimes he followed the track which leads from Lochaber into Badenoch and the valley of the Spey; but wherever he went marvels attended his footsteps. When chanting the evening hymns near the fortress of King Brude, he and his companions were molested by some Druids. The saint then sang the 44th Psalm, his voice pealing like thunder striking king and people with terror and amazement. When some of his companions had taken five fish in the river Sale (Sheil in Moidart), they were commanded by the saint to try again, and were promised a large fish. They obeyed the saint's command, and hauled out with their net a salmon of astonishing size.

In Lochaber the saint blessed the heifers of a poor man who had entertained him hospitably, and from that day the five heifers increased to 150 cows. In the same country he blessed a stake which killed wild beasts, but which could not harm men or cattle; and the happy peasant who possessed it was plentifully supplied with animals which were impaled thereon, until at the evil instigation of his wife he cut the stick in pieces and burned it in the fire. For St Columba'a alleged brush with the Loch Ness monster see the story that leads off Part Two of this book. Broichan, the Druid of King Brude, held in captivity a Scotic slave, and refused to set her free. The saint prophesied the Druid's death; but when appealed to in his illness, and being assured he had freed the slave, he restored him to health by causing him to drink water on which there floated a white pebble, which Columba had picked up in the channel of the river Ness. On Loch Ness "the long lake of the river Nessa," he sailed in his boat rapidly against the adverse wind which the

Druid Broichan had raised. While walking by Loch Ness, he was suddenly inspired by the Holy Ghost to go and baptise a heathen for whose soul angels were waiting. He came to Glenurquhart, and there found an aged man named Emchat, who, on hearing the word of God preached by the saint, believed and was baptised, and, accompanied by angels, passed to the Lord. The saint and his brethren seem to have penetrated every corner of Inverness-shire.

The Newcomers

Between the death of Malcolm Caenmore and the time of David I, the state of the North was one of constant insurrection. The former sovereign is generally supposed to have built a castle at Inverness upon the present site, but its governors seemed unable to exert much authority. The risings of the men of Moray were more numerous than we care to chronicle. With King David, a new policy was inaugurated — a policy which was carried out by his grandson Malcolm, by William the Lion, and by Alexander II. During the reigns of these kings the state of our northern county was entirely altered.

During the twelfth century there was a bloodless revolution in Scotland. A new people began to pour across the Scottish Border from the south, displacing the old inhabitants, encouraged by the king, and welcomed to the new home they had sought for themselves. There was a stream of English colonisation towards the Lowlands of Scotland. It was an extraordinary emigration, not like that of our Ayran ancestors, who moved in tribes, and not like that caused by the pressure of an overcrowded population. The new-comers belonged to the ranks of the aristocracy. They were of noble birth and knightly accomplishments — men of the sword, used to the court, the camp, and the usages of chivalry. Some of them were Anglian, of families settled long in Northumbria; most were of the

Norman race, which had come over with William the Conqueror.

These emigrants were cordially received by the king. It was doubtless thought that their culture and their skill in arms would prove useful in developing and defending the country, and it was reasonably expected that they would prove loyal to the sovereign to whose generosity they owed their fortunes. They received lands from him, which they held in feudal tenure; and they settled on the estates thus acquired. The natives gave way before them, or remained under their protection. Knightly Norman and Saxon lord built their castles, and gave lands to their followers under a similar title to that by which they held their own; and the feudal system became stamped upon the whole country. The system was a very simple one. The king was regarded as the owner of the whole land of the kingdom. He retained large estates in his own hands, from which he derived his personal followers and his royal revenues. The rest

The Royal army was victorious

he gave to his nobles, on condition that they should maintain for the defence of the kingdom a certain number of armed men. These tenants of the Crown followed the example of the sovereign. Each retained a portion of the land in his own hand, and bestowed the rest in estates of smaller or larger size on condition that each noble or knight who held of him should supply a portion of the armed force he was required to provide for the royal standard. Each knight, again, let his land to men of inferior degree on condition that they provided themselves with requisite arms, and assembled under his banner for military service.

These great changes in the South were viewed with apprehension by the men of the North. King David had only reigned six years when they rebelled against him, led by Malcolm, a natural son of his predecessor. Following Malcolm were the men of Moray, with their maormor Angus, now termed Earl of Moray, at their head. With 5000 men they entered Scotia. The commander of the royal army met them in battle and was victorious. He pursued them into Moray, and reduced again that ancient kingdom into subjection. The Irish annalists chronicle the fight: "Battle between the men of Alban and the men of Moray, in which fell 4000 of the men of Moray with their King Oangus, son of the daughter of Lulag." The changes that followed this battle were rapid, and all in the same direction.

David forfeited their territory to the Crown. He portioned it out to men who were strangers to the country, and who held their estates as vassals, according to Norman usage. Their fortresses rose throughout the conquered kingdom of Moray. Unlike the strongholds that preceded them — the raths, buildings of wood or wattles on the top of a mound protected by earthern works — these fortresses were of stone. They were not for defence but for aggression; each was a centre of royal authority, each a menace to the rebels of the district: the Comyn, a great Norman lord, held Badenoch and Lochaber with his castles at Ruthven and Inverlochy. Bisset, another Norman with lesser barons under him, dominated the Aird and

Strathglass from his castle at Beaufort. Durward, a third, ruled Glenurquhart and its neighbourhood from the royal castle on Loch Ness; whilst at Inverness itself there was a royal castle, held by a sheriff in the king's name, and visited often by the king in person.

The Rise of Inverness

The ancient inhabitants were thoroughly brought into subjection. If we may believe Fordun, Malcolm IV "removed the whole nation of the Moravianses from the land of their birth, as of old Nebuchadnezzar King of Babylon had done with the Jews, and scattered them through the other kingdoms of Scotland, both beyond the mountains and on this side thereof, so that not even one native of that land abode there, and installed therein his own peaceful people." How far this eviction of the old inhabitants was carried out, we have no means of knowing. It was probably but partial in extent, and confined to the border of the Moray Firth; but those inhabitants who remained were thoroughly under the dominion of their overlords. The *nativi,* as they were called, were entirely their property: they were serfs, the goods and chattels of their master. The castle rising in each separate district of Inverness-shire proclaimed the supremacy of the baron and the king.

But the castle and all it represented was not the only instrument by which our northern county was brought into harmony with the rest of Scotland. There were two other important feudal institutions planted among its people, which exercised upon them a great and beneficent influence. These were the Burgh and the Church.

It was part of the policy of King David I and King William the Lion to create trading communities in different parts of the kingdom — chartered corporations endowed with special privileges, and living under the protection and superintendence of the king. These royal burghs, as they were called, with the lands belonging to them, were his exclusive property, and generally they rose under the shadow of a royal castle. The inhabitants were vassals of the Crown.

The hamlet of Inverness with its noble and safe harbour was in every way suited to be a commercial centre. It was accordingly erected by the Crown into a burgh, and under the protection of the king a number of Anglo-Saxons, Flemings, and southern Scots settled there: the names of the early citizens testify to their foreign origin.

Inverness was probably made a royal burgh by David I; but its privileges were clearly defined and confirmed by King William the Lion, who granted four charters in its favour. By the first of these, the privileges of the town were extended to all the king's burgesses of Moray, and it was declared that burgesses were not liable to prosecution for any debt that was not personally their own. The second charter, dated 1180, granted land for the support of the burgh. It exempted all burgesses of Inverness from all tolls and customs throughout the kingdom, and prohibited anyone not a burgess from buying or selling within the burgh or in the shire. The king promised to make a fosse around the town, which the burgesses were to enclose with a good paling. The third charter confirmed to Geoffray Blund, burgess of Inverness, and his heirs, and to all the burgesses of Inverness and their heirs, exemption from the wager of battle, — "Perpetual liberty that they shall never have combat among them, nor shall any burgess or any other man of our whole kingdom have combat with our said burgesses of Moray, or with their heirs save on oath: moreover, I have granted to my said burgesses of Moray and their heirs that they make half the oath and half the forfeiture which my other burgesses make in my whole kingdom, and they shall be free of toll throughout my whole kingdom forever." The fourth charter appointed the Sabbath-day (Saturday) as the day for a weekly market, and granted the king's peace to all who should come to it. It granted to the burgesses all privileges enjoyed by those of other burghs of Scotland. It prohibited all without the burgh from manufacturing cloths, dyed or cut, charging the Sheriff of Inverness, should any such cloth be found, to seize it. It forbade buying or selling merchandise or keeping taverns in any place in the shire except the burgh, "unless in a town where a knight or laird of the town may be staying"; and it conferred on the bailies authority to enforce the observance of all its stipulations.

With the privileges granted in these charters the burgh of Inverness entered on its career as a commercial centre and an outpost of civilisation. The establishment of a free town, with privilege of trade and right of government by its own laws, marked a new era in the history of the Highlands. The burgh was the home of freedom. While the dwellers without the walls of Inverness were but serfs — hewers of wood and drawers of water to those above them — those within the burgh were free men; and by the laws of the burgh, as of all burghs in the kingdom, it was enacted that "if any man's thryll barouns or knikhts cumys to burgh and byes a borowage, and dwels in the borowage a twelfmoneth and a dey, frorutyn challenge of his lorde or his bailye, he shall be ever mare fre as a burges within that kingis burgh, and joyse the freedom of that burgh."

The position of the newly founded town must have been a very difficult and trying one to maintain, and it had many times to suffer from the assaults of the wild tribes among which it was placed. But its progress, if often interrupted, was steady. The burgh rose slowly but surely to a position of importance. In 1249, Matthew Paris, describing the armament which accompanied Louis IX on his crusading expedition to the Holy Land, speaks of the great ship of the Earl of St Poll and Blois — a "wonderful vessel" he calls it — which had been built for the Earl at Inverness. Even at that early period the Celtic village on the banks of the Ness had outgrown its primitive character, and had, under its new privileges, become the home of such labour and skill that there were found in it workmen able to fit out a great ship, whose beauty excited wonder and admiration amid the vessels manned by the chivalry of France.

But neither the influence of the Castle nor that of the Burgh affected Inverness-shire so powerfully as that of the Church.

The Church planted by St Columba and his followers had

apparently been brought, as regarded its doctrines and ceremonies, into conformity with the Church of Rome; but its general framework and polity werre peculiar to itself. It was a collegiate system. Its clergy lived together in communities, and in some central position, whence they went forth as missionaries to preach among the surrounding tribes. With the coming of the Normans and the feudalising of the North, this Church polity was changed. A parochial clergy superseded the missionary system that had formerly supplied the spiritual wants of the people. The monastic orders of the Church of Rome were introduced among them, and a bishop ruled over the territory which had formerly been subject to the jurisdiction of the Columban monastery.

The bishopric of Moray was founded by King Alexander I in 1107, but at that time the northern part of the kingdom was so disturbed that the bishop was unable to fix his residence there. It was not till the time of Bricius, the sixth bishop, in 1203, that the bishop became resident. His cathedral was at Spynie, and at his death it was transferred to Elgin. A great part of what is now Inverness-shire was within the diocese of Moray, and was included in the deaneries of Inverness and Strathspey. The rest of our county lay within the diocese of Argyle, the bishopric of which was founded in 1200; and the parishes of Inverness-shire were partly within the deanery of Lorn and partly within that of Morven. The whole of Inverness-shire was thus placed under the parochial system. It was one that touched very closely the life of the people. Each separate district had its resident priest, who discharged the offices of religion to those living within its bounds, and who was responsible for their superintendence. He was maintained by the tithes of the baron's land, of his corn, his pastures, and his fishing. Some of these parishes were erected and endowed by the Crown; others by the strangers who had settled in the country. Thus Kingussie was erected by a certain Gilbert de Kathern; Kiltarlity and Kirkhill by Bisset, Lord of Beaufort; and there were other territorial magnates who were equally munificent.

The conventual system of the Church of Rome was but slightly represented within the bounds of Inverness-shire, compared with other parts of Scotland. The monasteries of Pluscarden and Kinloss, not far from its southern border, and Beauly on its northern confines, were probably sufficient for the needs of the inhabitants. The Priory of Beauly occupied, until the Reformation, a conspicuous place in Inverness-shire. It was founded by John Bysset, Lord of the Aird, in 1230, and belonged to the Vallescaulians, or order of Vallis Caulium. It was one of the three monasteries of that order then existing in Scotland. The monks were men of austere lives. All property was held in common. Chapter was kept daily. Flesh-meat was forbidden in the refectory. For part of the year two meals a day were allowed: bread, water, and pulse formed the diet for the rest of the year. Sackcloth was worn next the flesh. Most of their time the monks spent in reading, prayer, and contemplation. They wore a white cassock with a narrow scapulary, and they never went beyond the precincts of their convent. The brethren were much occupied with gardening, and with the cultivation of the neighbouring lands belonging to them. The site of their house well deserves its name of Beauly, or, as it is called in the Latin charters, *Monasterium de bello loco*. It was placed amid the tract of alluvial soil brought down by the river, open to the sunny south, looking across to the wooded hills beyond the water, and surrounded by level land producing the finest wheat. The influence of the brethren must have been considerable among the wild tribes where their lot was cast. They held up before them for generations the virtues of a peaceful and self-denying life. They showed them what might be done in the improvement and cultivation of the soil. They received within their precincts the children of the neighbouring barons, and gave them such education as they were able to impart.

In the town of Inverness there was founded in 1233 a monastery of preaching friars of the order of St Dominic. It must have been a building of importance, and it was well endowed. It is said that Alexander II, when in Paris in 1217, saw

The monks showed them how to improve the soil

the founder of the order, and besought him to send some of his brethren to Scotland in order to teach the people, promising them all help and encouragement. It was in fulfilment of this promise that he founded in several towns in Scotland, as well as at Inverness, monasteries of the Dominican order.

Thus by the power represented by the Castle, the Burgh, and the Church, Inverness-shire was entirely feudalised, and Normans, Saxon Lords, and Flemings dominated the ancient Celtic inhabitants. How despotic their power was is illustrated by an agreement entered into between the Bishop of Moray and Comyn, the great Lord of Badenoch. In this agreement it is provided, in regard to the native men *(nativi)*, that the bishop should have all the cleric and two lay native men, but that all the other native men on lands in Badenoch, with all their chattels and possessions, and with their children and all their posterity, and the chattels of their children, should belong to Walter Comyn.

Hard times for Inverness.

In the early 18th century Inverness was a town of between 2000 and 3000 inhabitants. The number of houses in the burgh was probably between 400 and 500. In the centre of the town was the cross, which stood on the Exchange. Here converged four streets — East Street to the east, Bridge Street to the west, Castle Street to the south, and Kirk Street to the north. East Street extended from the cross to the Eastgate, while Bridge Street was its continuation westwards to the river. Castle Street did not run quite so far south as it now does ; while Kirk Street practically ended at the parish church. At the chapel-yard were the butts, where the citizens congregated with their arms in times of danger, or for inspection and exercise. Still farther to the north was the pier and what remained of the disused and partly dismantled fort of Oliver Cromwell. At the foot of Bridge Street the river Ness was spanned by a handsome stone bridge. On the west side of the river was a scattered hamlet of humble dwellings, which formed part of the burgh though they could hardly be said to be in it.

There were very few public buildings. The principal was the Castle, which stood on the site of the present building. It had been put in good repair and had been strongly fortified by General Wade, and commanded the town and the bridge over the Ness, the only bridge leading from the southern to the northern side of the Great Glen. Next in importance was the parish church. In its session-house the council met once a year to elect magistrates.

Near the cross, at the top of Bridge Street and Kirk Street, was the tolbooth, comprising the court-house and jail. At the ground-level under the tolbooth stair were two shops. The tolbooth had a steeple with bells and a clock. The steeple was taken down and rebuilt in 1691, part at least of the cost being met out of money collected to buy off Coll Macdonald of Keppoch when he threatened the town. The kind of building the tolbooth was may be gathered from the fact that it had no chimney until the steeple was rebuilt.

For the size of the town its trade was considerable. The greater part of the ground between Church Street and Academy Street was covered with malt-kilns and barns. A large and important business was done in malting. The privilege of engaging in this business was confined to guild brethren. The malt was sold to the people of the surrounding districts and paid for in hides, in the tanning and export of which another large section of the trade of the town consisted. In addition to the various branches of the building trades, and those necessary for supplying the everyday wants of the people, there were burgesses engaged in the trades of armourer and glover. Many of the merchants took part in transactions of considerable magnitude, and were men of substance. The well-known names of Cuthbert, Duff, Inglis, Robertson, and Forbes, familiar in local history, were those of Inverness merchants who acquired estates in the neighbourhood of the town.

At the period of "the '45" the town was considerably impoverished. The fiscal policy of the Government had inflicted serious injury on its trade. Its main industry, "malting," had declined, and other trades suffered from the consequent depression. Its import and export trade seems, on the other hand, to have kept up; for in 1738 a new quay, called the Citadel Quay, was built, which could at high tides receive vessels of 150 tons. The expense of erecting this quay was £2790, defrayed by a heavy excise on ale and beer used in the town, the collection of which excited great dissatisfaction among the inhabitants.

Mr John Mackey, whose travels through Scotland were published in 1723, and who visited the burgh probably about 1717, gives a pleasing account of Inverness. He speaks of it as "a pretty town situated at the mouth of the river Ness, which runs from a lake of that name full twenty-three miles long.

There are two very good streets in the town, and the people are more polite than in most towns in Scotland; they speak as good English here as at London and with an English accent, and ever since Oliver Cromwell was here they are in their manners and dress entirely English. Here are coffee-houses and taverns as in England. Here are the ruins of an old castle, and indeed the place deserves to be well fortified, for it is one of the most considerable passes between the low country and the Highlands."

Mr Burt, who wrote after the visit of this traveller, has nothing to say of the beauty of the situation of Inverness, and indeed is anything but flattering in his description of its streets and buildings. "Inverness," he tells us, "is one of the royal boroughs of Scotland, and jointly with Nairn, Forres, and Chanonry, sends a member to Parliament. The town has a military governor, and the corporation a provost and four bailies, a kind of magistrate, little differing from our mayors and aldermen. Besides whom there is a dean of guild, who presides in matters of trade, and other borough offices, as in the rest of the corporate towns of the country. It is not only the head borough or county town of the shire of Inverness, which is of large extent, but generally esteemed to be the capital of the Highlands; but the natives do not call themselves Highlanders, not so much on account of their low situation as because they speak English. Yet though they speak English, there are scarce any who do not understand the Irish tongue; and it is necessary they should do so to carry on their dealings with the neighbouring country-people, for within less than a mile of the town there are few who speak any English at all.

"The bridge," he says, "is about 80 yards over, and a piece of good workmanship, consisting of seven arches, built of stone, and maintained by the toll of a *bodle,* or the sixth part of a penny, for each foot-passenger with goods, a penny for a loaded horse, etc."

✗   GAELIC

The great Jail escape!

He does not appear to have a great opinion of the criminal administration of the burgh. "From the tolbooth or county gaol," he tells us, "the greatest part of the murderers and other notorious villains that have been committed since I have been here have made their escape, and I think this has manifestly proceeded from the furtherance or connivance of the keepers, or rather their keepers. When this evil has been complained of, the excuse was, the prison was a weak old building, and the town is not in a condition to keep it in repair; but, for my own part, I cannot help concluding from many circumstances that the greatest part of the escapes have been the consequence either of clan interest or of clan terror. As, for example, if one of the magistrates were a Cameron, the criminal Cameron must not suffer if the clan be desirous he should be saved."

It is not probable that any of the magistrates of Inverness would belong to the clan of Lochiel, but doubtless the peace-loving citizens had their own reasons for not offending any of the clans by which they were surrounded. Their town at this period was almost undefended, and it might be better for the magistrates to allow any captive Highlander to make his escape than to incur the wrath of some offended chief and his following.

The merchants and other men of business met at the cross for the transaction of their affairs. "They stand in the middle of the dirty street, and are frequently interrupted in their negotiations by horses and carts, which often separate them from one another in the midst of their bargains."

Dirt is the continual complaint of this Englishman. It meets him everywhere — in the houses, churches, streets. The last he allows to be well paved, but when he asked the magistrates one day when the dirt was almost above his shoes

Burt was critical of the state of Inverness streets

why they suffered the town to be so excessively dirty and did not employ the people to clean the streets, the answer was, "It will not be long before we have a shower." *

The houses appear to heve been built end on to the streets, with a staircase outside which led to each floor. The lowest stage of the building had a door towards the street which served for a shop or a warehouse. The suburbs of the town were made up of "most miserably low dirty hovels, faced and covered with turf, with a bottomless tub or basket in the roof for a chimney."

* OF RAIN

Style and manners

Of the shops, or, as they were called, warehouses, our visitor thought very little. "There is indeed," he says, "a shop up a pair of stairs which is kept by three or four merchants in partnership, and that is pretty well stored with various sorts of small goods and wares mostly from London. This shop is called by way of eminence *the* warehouse here (for the purpose)." To call such a place a warehouse, or its proprietor a merchant, evidently gives our narrator considerable amusement. **"On this side of the Tweed many things are aggrandised in imitation of their ancient allies (as they call them) the French. A** peddling shopkeeper that sells a pennyworth of thread is a *merchant,* the person who sent for that thread has received a *commission,* and bringing it to the sender is making a *report.* A bill to let you know there is a single room to let is called a *Placard;* the doors are Ports, an enclosed field of two acres is a *Park,* and the wife of a laird of fifteen pounds a year is a lady and treated with — Your Ladyship."

His description of the passers-by on a street of the town is graphic enough, though probably overdrawn. "In one part the poor women, maid-servants, and children, in the coldest weather, in the dirt or in the snow, can be seen either walking or standing to talk with one another, without stockings or shoes. In another place you see a man dragging along a half-starved horse, little bigger than an ass, in a cart about the size of a wheelbarrow. One part of his plaid is wrapt round his body and the rest is thrown over his shoulder, and every now and then he turns himself about to adjust his mantle when blown off by the wind or fallen by his stooping, or to thump the poor little horse with a great stick. The load in his cart, if compact, might be carried under his arm; but he must not bear any burden himself, though his wife has perhaps at the same time a greater load on her loyns than he has in his cart. I say on her loyns, for the women carry fish and other heavy burdens in the same manner as the Scots pedlars carry their packs in England. The poor men are seldom barefoot in the town, but wear brogues, a sort of pumps without heels, which keep them little more from the wet and the dirt than if they had none, but they serve to defend their feet from the gravel and stones."

The better class of the citizens, he says, were dressed in a more comfortable fashion: "The gentlemen, magistrates, merchants, and shopkeepers are dressed after the *English* manner, and make a good appearance. Their women of fashion go seldom abroad, but when they appear they are generally well dressed in the English mode."

Inverness was the only market town in the county. "There are four or five fairs in the year, when the Highlanders bring their commodities to market. But, good God! you could not

Goods on sale at fairs were
"of a most contemptible value"

conceive there was such misery in the island. One has under his arm a piece of coarse plaiding; these are considerable dealers. But the merchandise of the greatest part of them is of a most contemptible value, such as these — viz, two or three cheeses, of about three or four poundweight apiece; a kid, sold for sixpence or eightpence at the most; a small quantity of butter in something that looks like a bladder, and is sometimes set down in the dirt upon the street; three or four goatskins; a piece of wood for an axle-tree to one of the little carts, etc. With the produce of what each of them sells they generally buy something — viz, a horn or wooden spoon or two, a knife, a wooden platter, and suchlike necessaries for their huts, and carry home with them little or no money. You may see one eating a large onion without salt or bread, another gnawing a carrot, etc. These are rarities not to be had in their own parts of the country."

Dirt, laziness and poverty meet our visitor in every direction he turns. Nothwithstanding, however, his beggarly estimate of what he saw, there is no reason for believing Inverness was less deficient in the comforts of life than other Scottish, and even perhaps English, country towns of that period. There were, we know, men of good substance and education among its inhabitants, and there was a society into which it is evident Mr Burt was not allowed to enter. He had no military rank and no social position as a gentleman. He tells us himself that he was regarded as a spy. Perhaps, indeed, his exclusion from the hospitality of the well-to-do citizens has something to do with the contempt he so freely expresses. But his descriptions are amusing, and the contrast between the Inverness he saw and the beautiful town of the present day cannot but be gratifying. One thing he does allow to be worthy of praise. The Englishman was a man who evidently loved good living, and the materials for that were plentiful enough. "Salmon and trout just taken out of the river, and both very good of their kind. Partridge, grouse, hare, duck, mallard, woodcocks, snipes, etc, each in its proper season . . . . Wholesome and agreeable drink, I mean French claret, which is to be met with almost everywhere in public-houses of any note. French brandy very good, about three or four shillings a gallon. In quantities from hovering ships on the coast it has been bought for twenty pence. Lemons are seldom wanting here, so that punch for those that like it is very reasonable; but few care to drink it, as thinking claret a much better liquor. The little Highland mutton, when fat, is delicious, and certainly the greatest luxury, and the small beef when fresh is very sweet and succulent. Mutton and beef are about a penny the pound. Salmon, which was at the same price, is by a late regulation of the magistrates raised to twopence a pound, which is thought by many to be an exorbitant price. A fowl which they call a hen may be bought for twopence or twopence-halfpenny. Pork is not common with us, but what we have is good." It is evident our writer found Inverness a good place to stay in, and the abundance of creature comforts which he describes, and their moderate cost, might well detract to some extent from the sweeping criticisms in which he so freely indulges.

There was only one other town in the county besides Inverness at this period . . . Fort William. "It was erected," Burt tells us, "into a barony in favour of the governor of the fort for the time being, and into a borough bearing the name of Queen Mary. It was originally designed as a sutlery to the garrison in so barren a country, where little can be had for the support of the troops. The houses were neither to be built with stone or brick, and are to this day composed of timber, boards, and turf. This was ordained, to the end they might the more suddenly be burnt or otherwise destroyed by order of the governor to prevent any lodgement of an enemy that might annoy the fort in case of rebellion or invasion."

The cultured savages.

The inhabitants of the country outwith the two towns of Inverness and Fort William or Maryburgh were divided into three classes — the chiefs, the tacksmen, and the common people. The chiefs were the great men of Inverness-shire. They were all men of culture and education. They had all been trained at universities either at home or abroad. They could all speak English, Gaelic, and French with equal fluency. Their character and mode of living present us with a strange combination of culture and barbarity. A man like Sir Ewen Cameron, who could take his place in the Court of the king with grace, could yet head a pack of marauders to the South and return at the tail of a drove of lifted cattle. Keppoch, who had been trained at the university of St Andrews, was chiefly celebrated for his skill in tracking stolen cows. Chiefs possessed of a great degree of personal refinement and courtesy would without scruple indulge at will in deeds of lawlessness and ferocity. They seem to us to have been by turns cultured and courtly gentlemen, and wild savages bent on rapine and bloodshed. As their power depended on the number of their followers, it was their constant object to swell the ranks of their retainers and to keep alive among them the use of arms. When an English guest asked Macdonald of Keppoch the amount of his income, his laconic reply was, "I can raise 500 men." The importance and rank of each chief depended on the number of armed followers he could lead into battle.

The fighting strength of the Inverness-shire clans has been variously estimated. Probably the account given by General Wade in his report to the king may be taken as the most accurate. Lord Lovat could command 800 men, the Laird of Grant 800, Forbes of Culloden 200, Glengarry 800,

Clanranald 800, Lochiel 800, Keppoch 220, Mackintosh with the Farquharsons 800, Chisholm of Strathglass 150, the Macphersons 220.

The chiefs lived in considerable state. Each had a numerous household. A select bodyguard defended his person, and his visits were paid with much pomp and ceremony. He was accompanied by his henchman, his bard, his spokesman, his sword-bearer, the man who carried him over fords, the leader of his horse, his baggage-man, his piper and his piper's attendant. Mr Burt gives an amusing account of his meeting with one of these Inverness-shire magnates on one of his journeys. "On my way," he says, "I met a Highland

I met a Highland chieftain with his attendants

chieftain with fourteen attendants. When we came, as the sailor says, almost broadside and broadside, he eyed me as if he would look my hat off; but as he was at home and I a stranger in the country, I thought he might have made the first overture of civility, and therefore I took little notice of him and his ragged followers. On his part he seemed to show a kind of disdain at my being so slenderly attended, with a mixture of anger that I showed him no respect before his vassals; but this might be my surmise, yet it looked very like it."

The dwellings of the chiefs had little to boast of in the way of grandeur or convenience. Some of them still resided in their square towers or castles four or five storeys high. In such a rude retreat the Lord Lovat of the period of which we are writing is said to have entertained 400 people. Most of the Inverness-shire chiefs, however, had removed from their ancient fastnesses to houses built of stone and lime. These were, according to Mr Burt's account, "not large, except some few, yet pretty commodious."

Claret by the pailful.

In their homes the chiefs exercised unbounded hospitality. The provisions of life were abundant. Of butcher-meat there was ample store. His hills afforded the chief every variety of game, and his rivers abundance of fish. In an account of the housekeeping of Lord Lovat in 1590 we are told that the weekly expense of provisions in his household was seven bolls of meal, seven of malt, and one of flour. Each year seventy beeves were consumed, besides venison, fish, poultry, kid, lamb, veal, and all sorts of feathered game in profusion. The same abundance of good things existed in all the households of the Inverness-shire chiefs. Claret was both plentiful and good. It was imported from France. The consumption by Clanranald's house was twelve hogsheads a year. In that of Culloden the libations were of the most copious description. The custom of the house was to remove the top of each successive cask of claret and place it in the corner of the hall to be emptied in pailfuls. On the occasion of a marriage or a funeral the profusion was almost unbounded. The funeral of a chief was specially an event which called together people from far and near — all were made welcome, and all were sumptuously entertained. When The Mackintosh died in 1704 the funeral feasts and entertainments were kept up for a whole month. When The Chisholm died in 1817, his body lay in state for several days in an inn in Inverness, where wines and refreshments were laid out for all visitors. A banquet was held in a granary close to Beauly Priory, where he was buried. Those of "gentle kindred" occupied the upper room, while the commons caroused in the lower storey. Claret, it is said, "ran like ditch-water," and the old women of the village brought pails to carry off the superfluous whisky, and are said to have kept public-houses for six months afterwards on the relics of the feast. At the burial of Mrs Forbes of Culloden, her two sons and their friends drank so hard that when the company arrived at the churchyard they found they had forgotten to bring the coffin. /

The government of the clan by the chief was despotic, though tempered by the patriarchal relations between him and his people. Most probably all of the Inverness-shire chiefs had hereditary powers of jurisdiction. They could try and punish offenders against the law. Courts were regularly held and presided over by a person called a bailie, whose jurisdiction was absolute. He could fine, imprison, banish, and sentence to death. The tenantry of the district were obliged to attend the court of the locality, which was conducted with much pomp and formality.

The chief, though generally remitting the administration of justice to his bailie, often exercised his power to punish without the intervention of that official. When Mr Burt complained of incivility which he had received from some members of a clan, the chief at once said that if he would give him their names he would send him their heads. A Catholic priest having mentioned to Glengarry that he had occasion to rebuke and punish a well-known thief, that chief said the punishment was not sufficient. He ordered the offender to be cast into the dungeon of his castle and starved to death, a sentence which would have been carried out but for the intercession of the clergyman. Clanranald sentenced a woman who had stolen some money in his house to be tied by the hair to the seaweed on the rocks till the sea came in and drowned her. When ships about to sail for the West Indies came to Inverness, the neighbouring chiefs sent offenders from their various districts to be transported as slaves. No power but the strong hand could keep the people in order, and that power was freely exercised by their superiors.

When not engaged in looking after his estates and their management, the chief had other occupations. The chase was his favourite amusement. Red deer were plentiful in the hills, and other wild animals also were keenly sought for. Wolves had been at one time numerous, but were now extinct. The last seen in Scotland is said to heve been killed in Lochaber by Sir Ewen Cameron of Lochiel in 1680, but there is a tradition that it was slain in the parish of Inverness not far from the house of Kinmylies. There is also another tradition that it was slain by a woman in Strathglass. Wild cats, foxes, and badgers still abounded. The deer were not stalked as they are now, but were driven into a limited space, where they were killed by the chief and his friends with their broadswords. Sir Ewen Cameron entertained some gentlemen, whom he had made prisoners, with a hunting after this fashion at the head of Loch Arkaig. He was met, his biographer tells us, at the head of the loch by some hundreds of men whom he had ordered to be convened for the purpose. "These people, stretching themselves in a line along the hills, soon enclosed great numbers of deer, which, having driven to a place appointed, they guarded them so closely within the circle which they had formed round them that the gentlemen had the pleasure of killing them with their broadswords, which was a diversion new and uncommon to them."

But dearer to the chief than the pleasure of the chase was the raid made on some far-off country in search of spoil. To take a prey from the Lowlands was regarded as an innocent and healthful amusement. At the period of which we are writing the chiefs seldom ventured personally to lead a foray, for the restraints of the Government were very stringent. But most of them connived at their sons and the men of their clan engaging in the laudable pursuits of their ancestors, and shared without scruple in the proceeds of any successful venture. The Inverness-shire clans "most addicted to rapine and plunder", General Wade informs us, were the Camerons and the Macdonalds of Keppoch. They "go out," he tells us, "in parties from ten to thirty men, traverse large tracks of mountains till they arrive at the lowlands where they design to commit these depredations, which they choose to do in places distant from the glens they inhabit. They drive the stolen cattle in the night-time, and in the day remain on the tops of the mountains or in the woods with which the Highlands abound, and take the first occasion to sell them at the fairs or markets that are held annually in many parts of the country. Those who are robbed of their cattle follow them on the track, and often recover them from the robbers by compounding for a certain sum of money; but if the pursuers are in numbers superior to the thieves, and happen to seize any of them, they are seldom or never prosecuted. The encouragement and protection given by some of the chiefs of clans is reciprocally rewarded by allowing them a share in the plunder, which is sometimes one-half or two-thirds of what is stolen."

After the chiefs the class of people deemed most important in the county were the tacksmen. They were generally relations of the chief, and held, Mr Burt tells us, "pretty large farms, perhaps twenty or thirty pounds a year, and they again generally parcel them out to under-tenants in small proportions." The tacksmen were usually at this time men of some education. They were beginning to build for themselves stone houses, but many of them lived in turf huts not much better than those inhabited by the common people.

The state of the people generally, in comparison with

those of southern Scotland, was of the most miserable
description. Their number greatly exceeded the means of
subsistence afforded by the lands they occupied. The author of
an able pamphlet entitled 'An Enquiry into the Causes that
facilitate the Use and Progress of Rebellions in Scotland'
calculates that there was not at this period employment for
more than one-half the number of people in the Highlands: of
the remainder he says, "Many are supported by the bounty of
their acquaintances and relations, and the rest gain their
subsistence by stealing or robbery and committing depredations."
This account may be exaggerated, but there can be no doubt of
the wretched condition of the people compared with that of
their more southern neighbours, though doubtless it had its
alleviations. Their wants were few, from their infancy they were
inured to hardship, and they were in the main treated kindly by
their landlords. Eviction for non-payment of rent was unknown.
Though we may pity their state, they themselves, enjoying their
freedom, did not envy those dwelling beyond their glens and
mountains, and would have been sorry to change places with
them.

*Homes were very humble, with one end
reserved for the cows!*

Their houses were of a very humble description. They were built of round stones without any cement, thatched with sods and sometimes heather. Generally, though not always, they were divided by a wicker partition into two apartments, in the larger of which the family lived. In the middle of this room was the fire, made of peat, over which, suspended by an iron hook, was the pot for cooking. There was seldom a chimney, and the smoke found its way out by the roof and door. The other end of the house was reserved for the cattle and poultry. A Highland town, Burt informs us, was composed of a "few huts for dwellings, with barns and stables; and both the latter are of a more diminutive size than the former; all irregularly placed some one way, some another; at any distance they look like heaps of dirt."

Winter nights and summers in the shielings.

The family grew a little corn sufficient to yield them meal, which was their chief article of food; but they were often reduced to severe privations, and it was no uncommon thing for them in the winter season to be driven to support life by bleeding their cattle, mixing the blood with a little oatmeal, and frying the whole into a sort of cake. Their great dependence for a livelihood was not so much on their tillage as on their cattle. Great herds of black cattle roamed in the mountains. Each township had its own herd who looked after them. They had a few sheep of a small breed. Droves of horses belonging to the tacksmen and tenants were everywhere to be met with among the hills. They were hardy animals of small size, and were often allowed to run wild among the mountains till they were eight or ten years old, when they were hunted down and captured with difficulty. The people disposed of their stock to drovers, who collected their herds and drove them to markets and fairs in the Lowlands of Scotland and north of England.

Mr Burt seems to think that the people led a dull and melancholy existence: "They have no diversions to amuse them, but sit brooding over the fire till their legs and thighs are scorched to an extraordinary degree; and many have sore eyes, and some are quite blind. This long continuance in the smoke makes them almost as black as chimney-sweepers, and when the huts are not water-tight, which is often the case, the rain that comes through the roof and mixes with the sootiness of the inside falls in drops like ink." This seems cheerless enough, but we know that the Englishman was not correct in depicting the life of the people as dull. On the contrary, it was full of cheerfulness. When in the summer months they removed to their distant shielings, or in winter crowded round the blazing hearth, they passed their idle hours joining in the dance and listening to the song. They recited the legendary tales that came down from a far-off past. They sang the songs of their bards. They rehearsed the brave deeds of their ancestors, and they danced long and late to the music of the pipes. The Highlander of that time was far livelier, and his life was in some respects, notwithstanding its privations, brighter and more festive, than that of the Highlander of later generations.

The liquor of the tacksmen and people was ale, as that of the chiefs was claret. But whisky was beginning to be drunk, and stills were at work in many districts, tending to the demoralisation of the people. "The buddiell or aqua vitae houses" says a report of the time — "that is, houses where they distil and retail aquavity — are the bane and ruin of the country. These houses are everywhere, and when the price of barley is low, all of them malt and distil in great quantities." According to Mr Burt, the Highland gentlemen were immoderate drinkers of whisky, even three or four quarts at a sitting. In general the people that could pay for it drank it without moderation. In 1744 the town council of Inverness passed strong resolutions against smuggling, and against the use of tea and brandy, articles which they said had only begun to be used in this country, and threatened to destroy the health and morals of the people. The members bound themselves to discontinue the use of these extravagant and pernicious commodities.

Dress of the people.

The common dress of the people of Inverness-shire, and of the Highlands generally, has been fully described by Mr Burt. It is what he saw daily on the streets of Inverness and wherever he travelled about. "The dress consists of a bonnet made of thrum without a brim, a short coat, a waistcoat longer by five or six inches, short stockings, and brogues, or pumps without heels. Few besides gentlemen wear the *trowse* — that is, the breeches and stockings all of one piece and drawn on together; over this habit they wear a plaid, which is usually three yards long and two breadths wide, and the whole garb is made of chequered tartan and plaiding; this with the sword and pistol is called full dress, and to a well-proportioned man with any tolerable air it makes an agreeable figure. The common habit of the Highlander is far from being acceptable to the eye. With them a small part of the plaid, which is not so large as the former, is set in folds and girt round the waist, to make of it a short petticoat that reaches half-way down the thigh, and the rest is brought over the shoulder and then fastened before below the neck. The stocking rises no higher than the thick of the calf, and from the middle of the thigh to the middle of the leg is a naked space. This dress is called the quelt." Our Englishman makes remarks on this apparel which are particularly disparaging. But it is evident that no dress could have been better suited to the life the Highlanders had to lead. When they were obliged to lie out in the hills, in their hunting-parties, or in tending their cattle, or in war, the plaid served them both for bed and covering. The freedom of their limbs also enabled them to undertake long journeys and to climb the mountains much better than if they were clothed in modern apparel.

The common people of Inverness-shire were at this time almost entirely uneducated. There was a grammar-school at Inverness, but the Acts of Parliament ordaining that there should be a school in every parish had remained a dead letter. In 1709 the Society for the Propagation of Christian Knowledge in the Highlands was incorporated, and a few schools were planted here and there — one at Abertarff in 1711, and one at Glenmoriston in 1726. The progress of enlightenment is slow. It was specially so in this case, where only English was taught. It was long before any impression was made on the dark state of the county. Below the rank of tacksman there was probably no one in Invernes-shire who could sign his name or read a printed line.

We know but little of the religious character of the people. Ministers were in every parish, and kirk-sessions were active in maintaining discipline. The records of these bodies show how zealous they were in summoning offenders against morals, fining them for their shortcomings, and occasionally handing them over to the civil magistrates to be imprisoned or set in the pillory. There were only Irish Bibles used in the Highlands, and even these the people could not read. They were dependent for religious instruction on their preachers, who were few, and, it is to be feared, not of a high order.

But if religion lay light on the shoulders of the Inverness-shire man of the period, he was a firm believer in those things which are now termed superstitions. There were many in Inverness-shire at this time who were supposed to possess the mysterious gift of second-sight. Such were to be found in every parish. Witchcraft was also another article of Celtic faith. In 1690 the magistrates of Inverness applied to the Privy Council for a commission to try witches, and when Mr Burt at the table of an Inverness-shire chief ventured to argue with a minister against the probability of witchcraft being true, he was set down at once as an atheist. As late as 1704 two men were in durance at Inverness, "alleged guilty of the horrid crimes of mischievous charms by witchcraft and malefice, sorcery or necromancy." A commission, consisting of Forbes of Culloden, Rose of Kilravock, and some others, was ordered to take them on trial, and they were afterwards executed under care of the magistrates of Inverness. Fairies were still seen by the belated hunter, and every family of importance in the county had its special ghost.

Modes of transport

In the year 1800 it had been attempted to establish coaches between Inverness and Perth, and between Inverness and Aberdeen; but from the state of the roads at that period, and the little intercourse that then took place, it had been necessary to discontinue them after a short trial. It was not until 1806 and 1811 that coaches were regularly established in these directions. After the completion of the parliamentary works, they began to run from and to Inverness with great frequency. Forty-four coaches arrived at, and the same number departed from, Inverness every week. Postchaises and other modes of travelling increased proportionally. Instead of five postchaises, which was the number kept in Inverness about the year 1803, there were in 1828 upwards of a dozen, besides two establishments for the hire of gigs and horses, all of which found sufficient employment.

The number of private carriages at Inverness and its vicinity increased. In 1715 the first coach or chariot seen in Inverness is said to have been brought by the Earl of Seaforth, and was an object of wonder and veneration to the inhabitants. In 1760 the first postchaise was brought to Inverness, and was the only four-wheeled carriage in the district. Soon after the roads were finished there were four coach building companies in the burgh.

With facilities for travel, inns were established on all the principal roads, and in the remotest parts of the country the traveller found accommodation and the means of continuing his journey. Regular carriers for the conveyance of goods passed at all seasons of the year from one place to another. A postal service reaching to the extremes of the county was also established.

A great increase in the value of property took place almost immediately on the completion of these improvements. In Inverness and its vicinity the increase was in several cases tenfold.

Steamboat communications were established between Inverness and the west coast and Glasgow, as well as between Inverness and Leith on the east coast. "The increasing wants of the inhabitants of Inverness sufficiently prove their increasing wealth" concluded a report published in 1825. "Since their closer connection with the southern counties a rapid change has taken place in the general state of society. The manufacture of hempen and woollen cloths was started, churches and chapels of various sects were built, Missionary and Bible Societies established, schools endowed, an infirmary erected, reading-rooms established, subscription libraries set on foot, two newspapers instiued weekly, and a horticultural, a literary, and various other professional and philanthropical institutions were founded. Two additional banks were likewise instituted, three iron-foundries and three rope and sail manufactories commenced, an additional bridge was con-structed, the harbour was enlarged and improved, the town was lighted with gas, and all within the last twenty-five or thirty years."

One item of improvement is specially noted in the report. "In no instance is the benefit arising from facility of com-munication more apparent than in the establishment in 1817 of the great annual sheep and wool market at this central point of the Highlands, to which all the sheep-farmers resort from the remotest parts of the country. Here the whole fleeces and sheep of the north of Scotland are generally sold or contracted for in the way of consignments, and in 1818 upwards of 100,000 stones of wool and 150,000 sheep were sold at very advanced prices."

Glen Evictions

Despite the improvements in communication and increased prosperity people continued to emigrate in large numbers; later came the enforced evictions which accelerated depopulation of the glens. The early emigrants were in many instances men of means. They emigrated with the view of acquiring a position of independence abroad which they did not expect to obtain at home. The outgoing band was generally headed by a man in whom they had confidence. Many of them went to join colonies of friends and relations on the other side of the Atlantic. They were buoyant with hope. The earlier emigrations were to a certain extent comparatively cheerful. When Glengarry tried to keep his people at home, the poet Burns denounced him as a tyrant, and the Highland Society as in league with Beelzebub in preventing the people from making their escape from the slavery of their lords and masters. Those who left Inverness-shire in those days went forth bravely in search of freedom and independence. But the later emigrants had none of the spirit and the enthusiasm of the pioneers. They were the crofters whom the tacksmen had left behind, who were dependent directly on the laird, and when he forced them to emigrate they left their native land with heavy hearts.

The Glengarry evictions in 1853 were particularly traumatic. The estate was possessed by a minor, and his mother, the widow of the late chief, who managed it, determined to evict every crofter on her property and make room for sheep. They were all served with summonses of removal, a message being sent to them that they would be conveyed to Australia. Finally, as it was not convenient to transport them to that country, they were told that they would be taken to North America. Scenes of the most heartrending description ensued. Some who refused to go had their houses levelled and burnt to the ground; no

Burned out in the Glengarry evictions

mercy whatever was shown them. Whole families were left exposed to the weather without shelter of any kind.

At one time only two of the native stock remained in possession of an inch of land on the estate of Chisholm, which in the olden days was the abode of a numerous clan. In 1849 more than 500 souls left Glenelg at once. Glen Dessary and Loch Arkaig were swept bare. So the clearing of the glens went on, and sheep took the place of men over a wide district of Inverness-shire.

The Beauly pioneers.

The first Inverness-shire agriculturists were probably the monks of Beauly. The monastic orders devoted much of their time to agriculture. Their lands were always the best tilled in Scotland. The approach to a monastery anywhere in the kingdom could always be traced by the fertile fields around it. The woods, enclosed and protected, were of loftier growth, the meadows and corn-lands better cultivated. The population inhabiting the Church lands were more active, industrious, and prosperous than those on the lands either of the Crown or the feudal nobility. The monks of Beauly were no exception to the general rule. It was probably to them — to their labours and their teaching — that the neighbourhood of the Priory and the Aird of Inverness-shire owed that beauty and fertility which still distinguish those districts, and which is noticed by our earliest travellers. One of the few traditions of the conventual life on the banks of the Beauly that have come down to us tells of the fame of the brotherhood as horticulturists. They often, it is said, got six chalders of good fruit off their orchard, and the old minister of Kirkhill, writing in 1662, tells us that "he heard old men declare that one tree in the orchard paid the teind — that is, carried ten bolls of pears, which were shaken and measured in pecks and firlots, good ripe fruit." We may be sure that like labour and skill to that with which they tended their apple and pear trees were also spent on the land of which they were the owners.

But though the neighbourhood of the monastery was always an object-lesson to the rest of the county, it does not seem to have produced much effect. The clansman dwelling among the mountains was certainly no agriculturist. He was a soldier, and the sword came more naturally to his hand than the plough or the reaping-hook. The conditions of his life, not to speak of the character of the soil, prevented him giving much attention to the tillage of the fields. Glenurquhart, like the Aird, was always fertile and cultivated, but other valleys had little in this respect to boast of. A scanty and imperfect cultivation of corn was limited to detached patches of arable ground among the rocks. Cattle were the main resources of the tribe, and the acquisition of these the great object of their forays. Their precarious crops gave them wherewithal to bake their oaten cakes and distil their ale or whisky, and they sought nothing more. Their corn was produced with or without manure, as that could or could not be procured. When the land had been scourged by a repetition of grain crops till it could bear no longer, it was allowed to go waste till it gained what was called *heart* enough to allow it to be cultivated again.

Part Two
The Loch Ness Monster

Loch Ness is often referred to as the "Queer Loch" on account of the legends regarding its monster, which through ages is supposed to have disported itself on the surface of the water on calm days. In fact, there seems to be more in the monster story of Loch Ness than mere imagination.

In *The Life of St. Columba* a "great beast" is described in the river Ness. As St Columba lived in the early part of the sixth century, this means that the Loch Ness Monster is probably fourteen centuries old!

The ninth Abbot, Adamnan, in his book on St Columba, written in A.D. 670, tells how the Saint was once crossing the river Ness when he saw some of the inhabitants burying an unfortunate man who had been seized while swimming by the monster, and so horribly mutilated that he was dead before his friends could pull him out of the water. St Columba, on hearing this, ordered one of his companions to swim across the Loch. He did so, and the monster, scenting further prey, rose again to the surface. The holy man then raised his right hand, and making the Sign of the Cross in the air, invoked the monster in the name of God to "go with all speed." The beast was so terrified at the voice of the Saint that it sank instantaneously to its lair, and the swimmer returned unharmed to the shore.

Another legend, of later years, tells how a tinker and his dog took refuge one cold autumn night in a cave in the rocks below Abriachan on the shores of the loch. As the wind was chill, the tinker placed some pieces of brushwood across the mouth of the cavern in order to seal his humble dwelling from the icy blast. After cooking his supper the tinker was resting with his dog by the fire, when the dog started to growl. On removing the brushwood the tinker saw a huge monster with fiery eyes and long black body. His dog immediately rushed at

St Columba tells the Loch Ness monster:
"Go away!"

it and engaged it in battle. A long fight ensued, until finally the monster dashed towards the loch and plunged into its depths with an unearthly snarl, the dog fastening on to it as he sprang. Long did the tinker wait, but his dog never returned. On certain calm days (so the story goes) the surface of the loch is said to be violently troubled, due to the continued fight between the monster and the dog, as they rise to the surface, each struggling incessantly to loose the other's grip.

When we pass from fiction to facts, as authenticated by newspaper reports, it is hard to discredit the existence of a strange creature in the waters of Loch Ness.

One eye-witness who saw it one February afternoon in 1932 described it as being from six to eight feet long (other observers have said thirty to forty feet) with a broad humped back, a swan-like neck and a small head with a jaw filled with rounded teeth. This observer described the monster as "paddling" slowly up against the current, which was running very swiftly, as the river Ness was in heavy spate at the time.

One man viewed the monster as it was crossing the main road between Dores and Foyers. He narrated that it had a long neck, which first came into sight as it crossed the highway, followed by a bulky body; but he could see no tail. The creature appeared to be carrying a lamb or small deer on its back, and moved with a jerky motion.

Another person declared he was taken aback by seeing a huge beast "for all the world like a camel," as he left Dores Inn, appearing through the foliage on the east side of the main road, as it was growing dark. He said he saw it "waddle across the road" and down the bank in the direction of the loch, where he lost sight of it in the trees; but he distinctly heard a great splash coming from the direction of the water, shortly afterwards.

Other witnesses have described a serpentine head and neck protruding above the surface of the loch. On one occasion, the monster was observed for forty minutes through powerful field-glasses as it lay basking on the surface of the loch, and eight separate humps were counted on its back.

The late Sheriff Watt of Drumbruie, Drumnadrochit, emphatically stated he saw the monster on several occasions while fishing the loch.

The spoor of the four-toed amphibian, discovered on the southern shore of the loch and reproduced in *The Daily Mail* was believed to be that of the monster. With new evidence continually flooding in from sources that are unimpeachable, it becomes palpable that some beast of huge dimensions does actually inhabit Loch Ness.

The Legend of
An Cu Glas
The Phantom dog of Arisaig

Several centuries ago there were severe losses among the flocks in Morar and Arisaig. Shepherds kept vigil but failed to trace the marauders. One summer day, a crofter's wife left her baby outside her cottage in a cradle, while she went to the well to draw water — leaving her collie dog in charge. When the woman returned, she was horrified to find the cradle empty and the mutilated remains of her child strewn over her cottage pathway.

*Visitors have been confronted with
the terrifying apparition*

Believing the bitch to have been the culprit, her husband, on his return from work in the fields, dragged his dog into the woods, where he gouged out its eyes and beat it to death in a fit of rage and remorse, and afterwards returned and destroyed the litter of puppies.

Shortly afterwards, to his great regret, he discovered that his dog had been innocent. A black wolf was responsible for the crime.

Now, according to legend, a phantom hound is said to appear in the woods of Arisaig, seeking revenge upon mankind. Visitors to the district have been confronted with the terrifying apparition of a huge shaggy dog with blazing blood-shot eyes, walking through the woods towards nightfall. This phantom is locally known as "An Cu Glas" in Gaelic — "the Grey Dog."

A Room in Rothiemurchus

Some years ago, an old mansion-house near Rothiemurchus, Aviemore, was rented as a shooting-lodge by a family from Edinburgh. They were delighted with the house and its winding passages, crooked staircases and curiously-shaped rooms. One of the rooms, however, had not been used as a bedroom for some years, as "no one seemed able to sleep in it." An old manservant stoutly maintained that there was no ghost, but that the room was *"droch"* (evil). The room, however, was furnished as a bedroom, and assigned to one of the guests — a business man who declared he could sleep anywhere. The room had three electric lamps, and except for its quaint shape, seemed not in the least unusual.

The guest liked his quarters and sat smoking for a while beside the fire before going to bed. Soon a strange feeling of uneasiness crept over him, and a lamp on the window-sill seemed to have a hypnotic effect on him. He switched it off; then the others seemed to menace him, so that he broke into a cold sweat of fear. He put out the bed and table lamps, then went quietly to the door and opened it. A noise from another part of the house made him jump in panic, and as he turned back into the room the stove was blown out by an icy draught of wind. Terror-stricken, the man groped about in vain for the lights, then tried to reach the open door. The darkness seemed "peopled with malignant spirits," and on the way out he struck his head against the door. When he came to himself, he was on a couch in another room, with his head bandaged. The noise of his fall had aroused his host, who was anxious to learn what had happened. The guest shamefacedly told of his unaccountable

The lamp had a hypnotic effect .....

feeling of terror, but declared that he had seen nothing.

The old servant was pressed to tell if he knew of any sinister event attached to the room; he unwillingly related the following story:—

About two hundred years before, the house had belonged to a Highland laird whose only son was *"as a chaill"* (deranged) and had been confined in that room. One day he had escaped, and meeting a servant girl on the stairs, had attacked and strangled her, and afterwards had thrown himself downstairs to his death.

Crunar the cruel

About the year 1625, there was born at Kingellie in the parish of Kirkhill, near Inverness, a strong, robust, overbearing and cruel individual called "Crunar Fraser." He was endowed with more than an ordinary portion of physical strength which in these bygone days was considered of very great importance. Crunar Fraser carried his cruelty to such excess, however, that he became the terror of the country. His Chief saw in him the makings of a good soldier and got him a commission in the army. Shortly afterwards, he was sent to Ireland, where civil war had broken out. His stepmother, inwardly rejoicing at getting rid of such a wild character, accompanied him to Inverness and on coming to the bridge, she told him she intended going no further. Before bidding him farewell, however, she put a charm around his neck which she said would guard him against steel and bullet. "And how long will the charm last?" asked Crunar. "Until you see my face again," his stepmother replied. Believing that if he destroyed his stepmother on the spot the charm would remain with him all his days, he unsheathed his sword and with one mighty swoop, severed her head from her body.

On his arrival in Ireland, he joined his regiment, and it was not long before his courage, daring and skill placed him in an unequalled position. As an officer, he exercised his powers mercilessly towards all those of his enemies who were unfortunate enough to fall within his cruel grasp. No quarter was given to any who fell into his clutches. It is said that on one occasion when a beautiful young girl arrested for a moment his murderous arm as he was on the point of thrusting his sword through her husband, he stayed his hand only for a second, and then cruelly murdered her husband who was a gallant and brave officer. The lady was spared but only for the purpose of

He felt the fair lady's hand on his dirk

carrying her off to the Highlands as his bride. As he was returning from the field with the lady seated on horseback behind him, he felt the fair lady's hands on his dirk. He instantly killed her and threw her lifeless body into the stream over which he happened then to be passing.

Meanwhile at home, news of Crunar's warlike exploits spread throughout the country, and although there were many of his clan who were proud of him and lauded these exploits, there were also a great number who dreaded his return. Strangely enough, after his return to the Highlands, he settled down to the life of a quiet and peaceful farmer, much to the surprise of the inhabitants of the district who expected him to return a ferocious and bloody soldier.

Some time before his death a company of Irish soldiers stationed in Inverness, on learning that Crunar still lived, and that his abode was within seven miles of the town, decided to put an end to his existence and avenge the havoc he committed among their own people in Ireland. Crunar, who was warned of their intention, requested those around him to carry him out to the east end of his house in order that he could meet his enemies in the open. Crunar was only just able to raise himself on his elbow as he saw the Irish soldiers approaching about a quarter of a mile away. Filling his lungs to their full extent he gave a tremendous roar which re-echoed among the surrounding hills. Hastily the Irish soldiers retraced their steps, being of the opinion that Crunar was still a desperate and bloodthirsty warrior instead of a bed-ridden invalid.

Never again was Crunar Fraser interfered with and he died in peace at a ripe old age. Local legend has it that ever afterwards the house of Crunar Fraser was haunted. It has long since crumbled into ruins, and not a vestige of it remains.

Witchcraft and Satanic revenge

For centuries before the Reformation, Scotland, like the rest of Europe, was enveloped in a fog of superstition. For countless ages the belief in magic had been fostered chiefly through the agency of the mysterious cult of witchcraft, and this dark fraternity probably had its beginnings in the Old Stone Age. Associated at first with the adoration of the bull, it came in early Christian times to be regarded as the worship of the horned Devil or Satan, who warred against the Christian faith. This fiendish cult gathered around it an enormous mass of superstitious belief and was thought to bestow upon an individual amazing and unnatural powers.

When Queen Mary came to the throne witchcraft in Scotland was so powerful and dangerous that stringent measures had to be taken against its adherents. Actually the dregs of witchcraft and its rites were to be found in Scotland until comparatively recent times.

The records of Inverness Police Court show that in 1883 a woman named Isabella Macrae or Stewart, of Muirton Street, Inverness, who was charged with an assault, produced in her defence a clay image, or *crop creadha,* which she believed had been made by an enemy for her injury. The legs of the image had been broken, accordingly her own legs were wracked with dreadful pains. The puppet was about four inches in length and pins were stuck in its "heart." According to the late Lewis Spence, even later than this was the experience of a retired army officer, who dwelt in Glen Urquhart. This gentleman appears to have aroused the enmity of some of his humble neighbours for, about 1890, workmen engaged in making repairs near the front door of his residence found a clay image buried there.

The vengeful feelings of a day-labourer who had l dismissed by a farmer at Kirkhill, near Beauly, prompted him to fabricate a clay image of his former master and bury it near his dwelling. The farmer fell ill, and suspecting that the man had resorted to this barbarous act, dug in the ground about his house and unearthed the abomination, after doing which he recovered.

Even more absurdly superstitious was the belief that unless part of a farm or croft was fenced off and devoted to the Devil, evil would befall the soil and the cattle which grazed upon it. The portion thus reserved to the powers of evil must remain untilled or unploughed. As the name of Satan was taboo among the people and might not be mentioned, such a plot of land was usually spoken of as the "Guidman's Croft," the "Guidman's Fauld," or "Clootie's Croft."

The story is told of how a certain farmer resolved to bring such a patch, which had long remained untilled, under cultivation, but the moment his plough scored the soil one of the oxen to which it was yoked fell dead, slain by a supernatural arrow which came winging out of the blue.

Fear of ladders

Because in the past a ladder was one of the main pieces of architecture in a gallows, the person who walked under a ladder was literally walking "in the shadow of death," says an authority on folklore.

Originally the fear of walking too close to a ladder was the fear of ending one's life on the gallows — a not unlikely fate in the early 1800s when men, women and children were hanged for minor offences. Gradually the superstition has broadened to include any form of ill-luck.

Ladders are also associated with violent death. They were used in executions by burning. A witch was tied to a ladder which either stood over the pyre, or was lowered into it.

A quaint fishing custom "for luck" can still be witnessed on occasions at certain fishing villages. Before casting off the ropes, the skipper of a fishing boat may sometimes be observed stepping ashore to distribute a quantity of hard biscuits among those gathered on the harbour "to see the ships off." Thereafter the women and children rush to the pier head to throw coins on to the decks of the vessels by way of a luck bringer, as the fishing fleet steams out to sea. For the same reason, coins are often thrown to children in the streets at weddings.

The Evil Eye

Belief in the Evil Eye is a most ancient superstition. A villager describing it in the year 1902, reported that in the small township of Duthill in Inverness-shire "plenty of people round about us here have got the Evil Eye and hurt both cattle and people with it," while a student of folklore in Scotland, writing in the same year, stated that "interragatories show that it still exists in Caithness, Sutherland, Ross-shire, in Lewis, Harris, both Uists, Skye, Tiree, Islay," and other localities. It is said to be the possession of certain persons of envious disposition, whose glance holds a withering and injurious quality which, when directed upon the goods, cattle or children of more fortunate people, causes them to decay, or affects them with mysterious ailments so that they fall into decline or even perish.

Women were more generally thought of as the owners of "the ill e'e," as it was called in some localities, than were men. The usual victims of this withering optical beam were invariably the prettiest and healthiest children in a Highland village, the choicest cow in the byre, or the best pig in the sty.

The *"eolas,"* to give it its Gaelic name, was generally held to be a hereditary possession which descended from father to daughter, or from mother to son, and the belief existed that some kind of magical knowledge, or secret spell concerning its use and function, was imparted from one generation to another. A woman who lived in Tarbet, Ross-shire, about the beginning of this century told a collector of folklore how one of her sisters was nearly blighted in early youth by a neighbour who had the *"eolas."*

The lady who told the story was carrying her sister, then a small child, on her back and was proceeding along the highway in this manner when she was approached by an old crone who dwelt in the village. The hag pulled aside the shawl which the child wore around her head, disclosing her face, exclaiming as she did so, "What a pretty little girl!" Frightened, the girl ran off, and when the pair reached home the child who had been "overlooked" was found to be "very ill."

Her elder sister explained what had occurred and their mother, who had her suspicions, sent for the old hag who had done the mischief and reproached her with her work. The woman admitted her fault and administered a charm to the suffering little one, who speedily recovered.

A woman known as "Mary of the Sprains," because of her uncanny ability in healing such injuries, flourished in Islay about a hundred years ago and was regarded as a person of mysterious powers, whom it was not wise to offend.

Lewis Spence tells us that not so long ago a servant in Strathtay known as Jean, who attended to the needs of a local laird, discovered that the gentleman in question was possessed of the Evil Eye. He had to be persuaded not to go near his own cattle, for when he did so the cows gave no milk for some days afterwards. On one occasion the girl was carrying a "kebbuck" of cheese wrapped up in a small sack when she chanced to encounter her master.

"That's surely a fine cheese you have there, Jean," he exclaimed as they passed one another. Later, on taking the cheese out of its wrapping Jean found it cracked through and through by the power of the Evil Eye, which is said to be so potent as to split a millstone or wreck a large ship — as did the glance of Gilbride MacIntyre of Ruaig, in Tiree, an ancient Gaelic poem asserts.

In a cottage near Clunes, Inverness-shire, there used to be an interesting vessel of juniper wood hooped with copper. It was used in connection with the Evil Eye superstition prevalent in ages past.

Water drawn from a running stream over which the dead and the living had passed was put into the vessel and used to cure human beings and animals supposed to have been afflicted by the Evil Eye — generally by a witch. After gold and silver coins were dropped in, the water was sprinkled on the victim from head to foot, or head to tail, as the case might be, in the name of the Trinity. A mouthful of the water was then squirted into each ear and the rest of the water thrown over the subject of the cure. If, when this operation was completed, the coins adhered to the bottom of the vessel, the cure was certain to be successful.

Phantom Pipers

Five men of the Cameron Highlanders heard phantom bagpipes during an exercise in a blizzard over the 2500 ft Corrieyarrick Pass, towards the end of March, 1958. The five were waiting for 40 of the troops with transport and hot tea at the foot of the pass. The troops came into sight 15 minutes later, but their pipes had not been playing.

The first of the five to hear the ghostly music was Corporal John Smith, from Leeds. "I was sitting in one of the trucks with Colour Sergeant Eddie Kearney, smoking and chatting, when I suddenly heard the wail of the pipes in the distance. I said: 'There's the pipes, the boys must be coming,' and everyone listened. Then Sergeant Kearney and all the others heard them too."

"The squad came into view about a quarter of an hour later," said Sergeant Kearney. "We were waiting in a farmyard at Garvamore, about 12 miles from Newtonmore. When the men reached us, Major D J S Murray, training corps commander, said he had spotted my red sash two miles off.

" 'But we knew you were coming, sir,' I said, 'because we heard the pipes.' He was astonished, and said that was very queer, because the pipes had not played a note since they came over the top of the pass nearly fours hours earlier.

"Being a piper myself, I know the sound of bagpipes and I am quite sure that was what we all heard. We cannot explain it."

The whisky witch!

On the shore of Loch Linnhe, near Fort William, there once lived a laird noted for the contents of his cellar. One day he was surprised to find that his whisky was mysteriously disappearing. The servants were questioned, but he was forced to believe in their innocence. Since no one could suggest a feasible explanation, the laird suspected that witches must be at the bottom of the business, and determined to surprise them at their nefarious work.

One night he went to his cellar without a light and, with broad sword in hand, burst open the door, entered and closed it behind him. He then swung his sword right and left and felt that he had succeeded in wounding someone or something. Although the place was very dark there seemed to be the glare and flash of what he thought to be cats' eyes. When a torch was brought the only evidence was some blood on the floor.

The laird then hurried to the hut of a woman reputed to be a witch, whom he suspected of being a leader in the affair and, sure enough, found her in bed — wounded and bleeding. When he saw, lying on the floor, her right leg hacked off at the knee, he was convinced of her guilt. He was, however, at a loss to explain how a woman could assume the shape of a cat, vanish like a spark, and convey her severed leg home with her! But, as many Highland witchcraft tales reveal, this power would be simple enough to anyone well versed in the Black Arts.

The White Lady of the Rowan Tree

The bridge is still there in Glentruim and the sharp bend in the road is as dangerous now as it was 90 years ago. The old tree, which for years had a swarm of bees in its innards and gave many a sweet morsel for the few who knew how to get it, is no longer where it was; but the moon still shines through the trees on to the rock on the other side of the road. One no longer hears of the White Lady of the Rowan Tree; but there was a time, and a certain time too in each month, when the older folks round Catlodge in Badenoch would not travel along the road from Glentruim to Laggan and pass the bridge, tree and rock when the moon was full. The very horses refused on this particular night to go over the bridge and pass the rowan tree, but of their own accord would go lower down the stream and rejoin the road further on. Even the dogs yapped and howled at something which the human eye could not see, although several of the older people, both men and women, swore that they had seen the ghost-like figure standing against the rock with outstretched arms and in white raiment.

It is rumoured that one old worthy who was dared to pass the place on the night of nights, took up the bet, fortified himself with several over the eight and set off for home. When his nag would not go near the infamous place, he dismounted and stumbled on alone over the bridge, past the tree and there facing him in front of the rock was the Lady in White. What happened after this no one knows, but the next day he was found lying in a shallow ditch beside the road a quarter of a mile further along, with his horse grazing near at hand and he with his face in a small pool of water.

The story-teller determined to find out the mystery, chose

the night of the full moon, got to the spot early, sat down beside the "big tree" and waited. The night was still as still could be. Not a leaf trembled and not a sound disturbed the air other than a flying ant or a hunting beetle or the far-away call of a bird. In the mirky gloom of the surrounding trees the moon shone down on the rock and road in fitful glimpses, then all of a sudden a bright sheet of white light lit up the rock and there standing up in front of it was as real a figure of a woman with outstretched arms as one could wish to see alive. For a moment the observer was nonplussed and indeed mentally terrified. A cold perspiration crept over his body. The flash lasted for about five minutes and then vanished into normality.

The Grey Dog of Morar

For many years before his death, old Sandy MacDonnell, ground officer (to the late Sir Berkley Sheffield), at Meoble, near the head of Loch Morar, was in the regular habit of piloting the estate boat — a fairly large motor launch — backwards and forwards — eight miles up and eight miles down the loch to the Morar end, so many days a week. One day, in company with three or four passengers and a crew of two local stalkers, while cruising up the loch, he noticed a large grey dog running hither and thither on Eilean Allmha, a small uninhabited island, covered with wild holly, near Meoble, on the south side of the loch. The animal was not heard to bark or whine, but seemed to run about in an agitated and bewildered frame of mind. It was a mystery how a dog got there, but it was decided to sail over and take the beast on board.

On the way over to the island the animal could be clearly seen running in and out of low scrub and occasionally trotting along the bank, as if in search of someone or something. Macfarlane, the oldest member of the crew (a gillie, and a veteran of the First World War), whispered in Gaelic that it was a "droch aite," (an evil place). "It's no use, we need not trouble ourselves," he said, "for there is no dog there. What we have seen was a warning, a spiritual warning." Anyhow, the boat was moored and a thorough search made of the whole place; but not a living creature — man or beast — was found.

On the way back to the anchorage at Meoble, the old man, whose countenance had now changed to one of ashen grey, repeated the legend that the ghost of a large grey dog always appears on that island near Meoble, on the south side of Loch Morar, shortly before a member of the Gillies or Macdonnell Clan dies. Old Sandy Macdonnell, skipper of the boat, passed away very shortly afterwards.

Loch Morar itself is the deepest freshwater loch in Scotland and is some 12 miles long. It is said to harbour a monster even larger than that in Loch Ness. I heard the legend of The Grey Dog of Morar while staying at Meoble prior to the outbreak of the Second World War.

Many years ago, one Donald Gillies went away to the war. His favourite dog, a grey bitch, somehow or other got stranded on Eilean Allmha. She had a litter of pups there, and they grew up as savage as wolves. When Donald came back, he went over to the islet to collect his dog. She fawned on him — but the pups, who had never seen a human being before, tore him to pieces. Ever since, the ghost of a grey dog is said to manifest when a Gillies or Macdonnell dies.

Another story I gleaned from a local stalker, Angus MacKellaig, of Morar, who had the sheep grazing on the mountainous ground at the head of Loch Morar. Kinlochmorar House had eight rooms. Only one was used. Angus spent his nights there on his occasional visits rounding up sheep. The other rooms were damp and dead. When I accompanied Angus one day on his rounds, he said: "I would not be surprised at all were we to hear barking of dogs and strange footsteps." Pressed for some explanation, he continued: "Well, now, it would be some years ago that Johnny Gillies brought up an Edinburgh lady on holiday. She went for a walk to the house, and as she got closer to it, she distinctly heard the sound of dogs barking inside it, as if they were shut up and wanted out. She was puzzled, for the house had been shut up for over thirteen years. When she got nearer to the building, the barking grew louder and louder; but when she opened the door, there was a deathly silence. The only thing she was met with was the breaking silence of an empty house. Last year a family of six persons all heard the same dogs barking, yet there wasn't a dog within miles of the place. It's all very strange; I don't know what causes them to bark, at all."

Part Three

Secrets of the Whisky Smugglers

By Francis Thompson

For as long as people have wanted commodities but have found them in short supply, or expensive to obtain because of State duties, the smuggling trade has ever stepped in to fill the breach. It has done this for centuries and is, as the newspaper headlines tell us, just as active today; though the present day goods 'run' into this country are more typical of our contemporary scene — from drugs and watches to aliens.

Inverness and its environs have a firm place in this story. So general was smuggling in Inverness at one time that there were two or three master coppersmiths who had the sign of a whisky still above their shops, indicating their employment. Eventually, after the Act was passed which authorised small stills to be established in the Highlands, so that good whisky might be legally manufactured and procured, a Revenue cutter was stationed at Inverness and another on the west coast, whose armed men traversed the countryside to put an end to smuggling.

Vessels from the Continent often anchored in the Inverness Firth to wait for a pilot or a favourable turn of the tide. The occasion was an opportunity for running into the nearby shore goods which were not destined to be unshipped at the harbour. Inverness merchants as a rule traded with Rotterdam for goods such as silks and brandy, and, in order to evade the heavy duty imposed on such articles, they found it more 'convenient' to have their consignments landed at Petty Beach (about 5 miles east of Inverness) and taken to Inverness by road without the knowledge of the Excisemen.

*A fleet-footed runner started for Inverness
with the "Petty Snuff Box"*

One 'respectable' Inverness merchant for a long time used an ingenious plan by which he got his goods smuggled to his shop. As soon as a ship from Holland arrived in Petty Bay, a fleet-footed runner started for Inverness with the news. This messenger simply handed over to the merchant an empty snuff box (it came to be known as the Petty Snuff Box) who then handed it back to the messenger, full if he was ready to take away the goods next day; or half-full, if the goods were to be hidden for a time. Often this procedure was carried out under the noses of unsuspecting Excisemen.

Once a large cargo of gin, brandy, tea and tobacco was landed at Petty Bay near Alturlie Point. The Chief Excise Officer at Inverness did not hear of this until eight days afterwards by which time all the stuff had been taken away. But a small portion of the goods were later recovered, valued at £1,000, which left the officer wondering just how much had slipped into Inverness under his eyes. Occasionally the Revenue cutter apprehended ships and on one occasion in October 1824 she arrested a lugger which had just landed 150 gallons of gin.

One of the boldest smugglers was the Factor for Petty, Bailie John Steuart of Inverness. He was a merchant on an extensive scale. He had more than a dozen ships sailing to and from the Continent. He bought up large quantities of grain, salmon, codfish and herring from all over the north of Scotland, found markets for them in foreign ports, and had his ships return with salt, brandy, wines, iron, copper and timber and with an endless variety of small merchandise luxuries which were extremely difficult to obtain at home. In May 1729 his barque 'Christian' landed a quantity of brandy near Petty which he transferred to his home at Castle Stuart. The Chief Officer of Customs at Inverness heard of the 'run' and sent his men to batter down the castle door to recover the goods. Despite his wealth, Steuart was a man who ventured too much and trusted too much. He died in poverty in 1759. He was of royal descent: from the family of Steuarts, Barons of Kincardine, in Strath-spey, founded by a son of the Wolf of Badenoch, who was a descendant of King Robert II.

Moonlight and Moonshine

Perhaps, like many another aspect of the laws produced by successive Governments, it was the various Acts of Parliament which caused the beginning of a full-scale and flourishing industry of illicit distilling in the hills, glens and remote places of the Highlands. Among the reasons for the Government interest in whisky-making was the understandable possibility of tapping into a rich source of revenue. But collection of the revenue was difficult and in some remote districts it was quite impracticable. A licence system was adopted which was based on the quantity of wash that could be used by a still, and presumed that a given quantity must yield a given percentage of spirit. This took no account of the actual gravity of the wash. Nor was account taken of the crude high gravity and saccharified wash that was commonly used by English distillers, compared with the weak natural wash favoured in Scotland. In Scotland the product of the still was for consumption without adulteration or artificial flavouring of any kind; whereas in England the distiller produced a coarse spirit for recitification, a further distilling mixed with various essences. The Wash Act of 1788, an Act of illogical thought, was replaced by a further Act, which was based on further misunderstandings about how stills produced spirits. The cost of licences was fixed at 50p in 1786; but this increased rapidly and by 1803 it was £163.

To get round the injustice of legislation, illicit distilling went on apace with the Government's attempts to tap off some of the revenue that flowed into the growing distilling industry. By 1814 the licence system based on the size of the still was discarded in favour of a system based on the wash and spirit, with a licence of £10 for the privilege of distilling. But another bureaucratic blunder was on the way: stills of under 500 gallons were prohibited, which meant that virtually all small home brewers and distillers in the region suddenly found themselves on the wrong side of the law. Colonel Stewart of Garth speaks of the iniquity of the 1814 Act in respect of the Highland area:

"It is evident that this law was a complete interdict, as a still of this magnitude would consume more than the disposable grain in the most extensive county within this newly drawn boundary: nor could fuel be obtained for such an establishment without an expense which the commodity could not possibly bear. The sale, too, of the spirits produced was circumscribed within the same line (Highland distillers were not allowed to market their spirits south of the Grampians), and thus the market which alone could have supported the manufacture was entirely cut off . . . . Thus, hardly any alternative remained but that of having recourse to illicit distillation. These are difficulties of which the Highlanders complain heavily, asserting that nature and the distillery laws present unsurmountable obstacles to the carrying on of a legal traffic. The surplus produce of their (farmers and tenants) agricultural labour will therefore remain on their hands, unless they incur an expense beyond what the article will bear, in conveying so bulky a commodity (grain) to the Lowland market as the raw material, and the drawback of prices on their inferior grain. In this manner, their produce must be disposed of at a great loss, as it cannot be legally manufactured in the country. Hence they resort to smuggling as their only resource. If it indeed be true that this illegal traffic has made such breaches in the honesty and morals of the people, the revenue drawn from the large distilleries, to which the Highlanders have been made the sacrifice, has been procured at too high a price for the country."

Another comment in the *Old Statistical Account of Scotland* (1796) was: "Distilling is almost the only method of converting our victual into cash for the payment of rent and servants, and whisky may, in fact, be called our staple commodity."

A fishy tale!

In time, in the Highlands at least, the term 'smuggler' came to be more associated with those who operated small illicit stills, rather than those who attempted to run foreign goods across remote shorelines for profit.

It was perhaps inevitable that a great fund of stories about exploits, near escapes and captures, seizures and encounters with Excise Officers grew to make illicit stills the subject of everyday conversation and reportage in the newspapers of the day. Writers on the Highlands and Islands in the past 150 years never failed to mention the topic in their books and, indeed, perpetuated as many myths and legends as true stories of the smuggling days of last century.

Often ingenious methods were used to thwart the attempts of Excise officers to discover both stills and spirits. On one occasion a band of smugglers were on their way from Glen Urquhart to Inverness with a consignment of whisky when they received word that a number of Excise officers were waiting to intercept them in the vicinity of Loch Ness. Determined to deliver their precious cargo to Inverness at all costs, the smuggling party split into two groups, one of which went ahead with a few barrels of herring as a decoy. The Excise officers were completely taken in and while a battle raged over the herring barrels, the main group slipped by with the whisky unnoticed.

Because of the ever-present need to escape detection, the smuggler or whisky-maker had to resort to many ingenious methods which would allow him to distil spirits in both peace and quantity; in addition, it was a fact that the longer the time he had for the process of distillation, the better the quality of his final product. An observer at the beginning of the 19th century says: "Everybody, with a few exceptions, drank what was in reality illicit whisky — far superior to that made under the eye of the Excise — lords and lairds, members of Parliament, ministers of the Gospel and everyone else."

Despite the fact that their production methods bordered on the primitive, the smugglers were well versed in the principles and intricacies of distillation. Generally, the nearest burn or stream served as a steeping vessel, in which they left sacks of barley for a couple of days to soften the hard starch of the grain. Thereafter, it was laid out to germinate in a loft, an out-house, or in what were called 'malt-caves' well away from prying eyes. For a period of seven to ten days, the swollen barley had to be turned and spread every twenty-four hours. Once the required stage of germination had been reached, the barley, or malt, was transferred to a peat-fired kiln to dry; this process checked further growth by withering, and also served to impart a delicious and peaty fragrance to the malt.

The stage called 'mashing' was simply tipping the dried malt into a cauldron or drum containing hot water and a layer of heather for draining purposes, and boiling it up for a couple of hours over a peat fire. The resulting fermentable worts were then carefully drained into a home-made fermenting vessel, and the process of mashing was repeated for a second time using fresh water on the original grains.

Mashing took up the best part of five hours. When the process was completed, a small quantity of barm was put into the fermenting tub and left for two or more days until the fermentation was completed. Then the distilling took place.

Most bothies had a single still and cooling worm; this meant that the actual distilling had to be carried out in two stages, the still having to be thoroughly cleaned between alternate charges of wash and low wines (the distillate resulting from the first distillation). The re-distillation process was critical and required all the smuggler's intuition and ingenuity to produce a high-quality product.

The most expensive part of the still was the 'worm', which was a coiled copper pipe which condensed into liquid the hot vapour from the wash-still and then passed it into the spirit-still. When this pipe became worn out, the smugglers used to dismantle all their equipment, but leave the worm. They then went off to the nearest Excise Officer and reported the finding of a still, whereupon they received their £5 reward. With the money thus acquired the smugglers would buy a new worm and set up a new still in another glen.

Inevitably smuggling bothies were dark, smoky and unhygienic places. The typical still had no head elevation, with the result that fuel oils, acids and other harmful impurities passed over with the alcoholic vapours into the cooling worm. Often this led to inferior, and indeed, dangerous spirits being offered for drinking.

Camouflaging was so important that bothies were difficult to find. The story is told of how one smuggler was shocked to find a local gamekeeper reclining on the heather-topped roof of his still-house. Another smuggler constructed his chimney in such a way that the issuing smoke blended with the spray of a waterfall.

Predictions of the Inverness seer

There are few people in the Highlands who have not heard of Coinneach Odhar, the Brahan Seer.

Even visitors to the region cannot fail to pick up the odd story or two about this prophet, this man who foretold the Highland future, yet who was a shadowy figure flitting on the very edge of historical fact and whose existence has not yet been proved beyond all reasonable doubt.

He is, however, only one name in a number who were real people in their time and whose existence and utterances about the future have been recorded.

One Highland seer who has tended to be overshadowed by the popularity of the Brahan Seer is the Rev John Morrison, a Minister of Petty parish, near Inverness.

In Morrison's case, being an historical person, his utterances were often noted and recorded, and as such are distinctly more authentic than those prophecies of the Brahan Seer.

They were included in both the oral and literary traditions of the Highlands and are taken as being further proof of the ability of certain Highlanders to operate on a plane which easily warped time and brought the future into the eye of the present.

One of the best known utterances of Morrison relates to a large stone, weighing some 8 tons, which marked the boundary between the estates of Lord Moray and Culloden.

During one of his sermons, he suddenly exclaimed: "Ye sinful and stiff-necked people, God will, unless ye turn from your evil ways, sweep you ere long into the place of torment;

and, as a sign of the truth of what I say, Clach Dubh an Abhainn, large though it be, will be carried soon, without human agency, a considerable distance seawards."

There was nothing so unlikely to happen. Yet, 26 years later, the stone was moved and carried out to sea a distance of 280 metres.

In a guide book to the Highlands it is recorded: "... an immense stone .... was, on the night of Saturday the 20th February, 1799, removed and carried forward into the sea about 260 yards .... more probable opinion is that a large sheet of ice, which had collected to the thickness of 18 inches round the stone, had been raised by the tide, lifting the stone with it, and that their motion forward was aided and increased by a tremendous hurricane which blew from the land."

A happy dance at the roadside

Morrison also predicted the clearances which were to depopulate the parish of Petty: "Large as the Ridge of Petty is and thickly as it is now peopled, the day will come, and it is not far off, when there will be only three smokes in it, and the crow of the cock at each cannot be heard, owing to the distance, at either of the others. After a time, however, the lands will again be divided, and the parish of Petty become as populous as it is today."

Another well-known instance of Morrison's faculty occurred when a number of women from Fisherton, in the Petty parish, had gone to Inverness to sell fish.

Before returning home they invested some of their cash proceeds in liquid refreshment and were thus the worse for wear when they passed by Morrison's manse.

Morrison went out to meet them, carrying a fiddle; on seeing him, one woman asked him for a few tunes. He complied and in no time at all there was a happy dance going on at the roadside.

The church elders, after the incident, took a dim view of his conduct and rebuked him.

But Morrison replied: "How could I refuse to play a tune for the woman who asked me to do so? The holy angels themselves will before long tune their harps for her .... her soul will this week pass into glory." The woman in question took ill within the week and died.

The full moon, taboos, brose and bannocks

The reflection of a people's beliefs, their attitudes to ancient traditions, and their stance on matters affecting individuals in a community, or the community as a whole, is to be found in no surer mirror than in the calendar of events kept throughout the whole year.

The twelvemonth cyclic period in human lives, with its four internal changes, is the hook onto which is hung the old clothes of one's ancestors, kept up to date by shifts in emphasis as the community's history is altered by internal and external influences and events.

The following short tour through calendar observances reveals the substance of the lore of Highland folk.

The time of Lent was 'Am Traisg', the time of fasting.

This was an important date in the calendar for a number of reasons.

In past years, time was counted by church festivals, the priest being the time-keeper for his parish; there was a calendar at the beginning of his service-book, and so the community came to him for their chronology.

In many parts of the Highlands which remained Catholic long after the Reformation, the socket of the Pastoral Candle, and even the candle itself, was used to advertise the approach of significant times; this reckoning succeeded the older folk-reckoning which was based on the same luminary, the moon.

One Gaelic mode of calculation was "Seven short weeks from Shrove-tide to Easter."

When the full moon of Shrove-tide came a few days after

St Bride's Day, it was known as a time thought to bring evil to any greedy person.

It was, too, a time for prognostication; for nut-burning and marriage divination, for putting symbolic articles in brose and on cakes specially prepared for the occasion.

It was an important time for the saining or protection of cattle. Various rites were conducted to keep the beasts free from harm.

In the central Highlands matrimonial brose was a savoury dish generally made from the bree of a fat jigget of beef or mutton. Before the bree was served on a plate, a ring was mixed in with the meal, which it was the aim of each eater to win.

After the brose came bannocks, enough to satisfy all the young people present at the feasting and with sufficient symbols shared out to make all happy.

In baking the bannocks the baker had to remain silent until they were cooked; one word could destroy the divination properties of the whole batch.

One cake was given to each person, who then slipped off to bed quietly with it; sleeping with one's head on the bannock could provide one with the sight of a future partner in a dream.

The sun was believed to dance at its rising on the sixth Sunday in Lent, which is Palm Sunday.

Good Friday was of particular significance; many taboos were recognised.

No iron, for instance, had to come into contact with the ground.

It was expressly forbidden to plough on Good Friday, though potatoes could be planted with a wooden dibble, and the ground raked over with a wooden-toothed rake.

So great was the aversion to doing any ploughing that there was, in some areas, a permanent prohibition on every Friday.

If a burial had to take place, the grave had to be opened the previous day and the earth settled over the coffin with a wooden shovel.

No blacksmith could work on Good Friday, because the nails of the Cross were said to have been made on that day.

It was a popular belief that those born on Good Friday had the power of seeing spirits and of commanding them.

The festival of Beltane, the Fire Festival, was of special importance, particularly in its connections with what was once popularly called 'fire worship.'

The celebration of Beltane on the first day of May was significant as being a good time for the propitiation of the elements, particularly the sun, to influence the growing crops.

Cattle were made to pass through the smoke of the Beltane fires so that they might be cleansed of any evil spirits which might bring them disease during the ensuing year.

The 'Taine Eigin', the fire of need, was lit on this day (after all the fires in the community had been extinguished) and from its new flames all house fires in the community were re-lit.

Deeply embedded in this festival was the belief that at this time, the welcoming of summer, there was a grand anniversary review of all witches, warlocks, fairies, wizards and other spirits and spirit controllers, to which new entrants were admitted.

Rowan tree and red thread ....

Such a congregation of evil was much to be feared and it was thus essential that every ritual was carried out in the right manner to ward off any ill effects from the annual convention of evil; rowan twigs, tied with red thread and made into crosses, were inserted into door lintels; and Beltane bannocks were baked and distributed to the children.

Beltane bannocks were made like oatcakes, in the usual way, but washed over with a thin batter of whipped egg, milk and cream, and a little oatmeal.

Like its counterpart in the Celtic year, Samhainn, in November, the origin of Beltane cannot be traced to ecclesiastical sources.

Like the names for February (the storm month) and July (the hot month) they predate Christianity.

Beltane was essentially the opening day of the year, when the rigours of winter were finally cleared away and the months ahead showed promise of warmth and fertility.

Its arrival signalled a wide range of activities such as releasing the cattle for their trek to the summer pastures among the hills.

A churning of butter was necessary, as was the making of a cheese, before sunrise on Beltane, to ensure that the fairies were kept away from the household produce.

No fire was given out on this day (or indeed on any other first day of a quarter of the year), for fear that the borrower might be given the power to spirit away milk from the lender's cows.

Samhainn, Hallowmass, is the first day of winter and was in

some ways even more important than Beltane, for it was a time when the work of the year was drawing to a close and preparations had to be made for the coming coldness.

In addition, the spirits which had blessed the crops and flocks now required payment by the observation of ritual.

All the fruits of summer were gathered in and set aside until the following spring, to the accompaniment of both ceremony and play.

The children gathered anything to hand for a bonfire, usually built on some rising ground and lit in the evening.

The sun, having done its work during the previous months, was now to be replaced by symbolic man-made heat and the fires represented this new reliance on self rather than on nature.

Among the games played were those thought to have some divination element in them; to see who would be married the following year, whether trade was to be fair, and what lay ahead in terms of life and death.

Today, many of the customs associated with Hallowe'en owe their currency to these past activities of former years.

At the very end of the year, the days of Yule were fully charged with import, including as they do Christmas, Hogmanay and the various saints' days.

In the Highlands, the seven days from Christmas to New Year were called 'Nollaig'.

No work was done during this time; rather, folk gave themselves up to friendly activities, offering both words and deeds of good will towards neighbours.

Christmas Day was 'Latha Nollaig Mhor', the day of Big Nollaig, and the night before it was 'Oidhche nan Bannagan', the Night of Cakes.

New Year's Day was known as the Day of Little Nollaig; its Eve was 'Oidhche nan Calluinnean', the Night of Blows.

Hogmanay was better observed than Christmas, mainly because of the former's place in the calendar: the old year was leaving its mortal coil and the new year was to be born to hopes of a new life, better prosperity and an improvement in the lot of whomsoever wished to have times better than those experienced in the departing year.

Thus, while Christmas was duly accepted for its message of hope, Hogmanay was of more immediate concern because it affected life and the material things around it.

New Year's Day was preceded by Calluinn, which was observed by playing games like shinty and making the preparations for a procession round the houses of the township.

At each house, a train of men and boys, though latterly the tradition was kept up by boys only, knocked on the walls of houses and, going sunwise, chanted a request for gifts.

The main feature of the procession was that the leader's head was enclosed within the hide of a cow, which was periodically struck like a drum by his companions; hence, the Night of Blows.

The 'gifts' received were the hospitality of the household: bread, cheese, oatmeal, and a dram of whisky for the men.

The present-day tradition of first-footing, taking something round with one to eat, to drink, and something for a fire, stems from these early customs.

Indeed, the present, for all its modern sophistication, is not so far removed from the past of our forebears.

New Year's Day in the Highlands was the Day of Little Christmas, its advent being celebrated by all in the household taking a dram and then a spoonful of half-boiled sowens — the poorest food imaginable. It was taken for luck.

This particular custom was common in south Inverness-shire.

Salutations of the season were offered.

A game of shinty was the order of the day for boys, as, indeed, it still is, or football, which is the modern equivalent — or else a 'sair heid' round of golf on the course.

As for the housewife, she had a long list of rites to perform.

Nothing was allowed to be put out of the house on this day, neither ashes, sweepings, dirty water, however useless or however much its retention in the house might cause inconvenience.

It was a serious matter to give fire out of the house.

The first person to enter the house was an omen of what the New Year would bring.

The 'first foot' was best if he were a young man bearing a gift of food, drink, or fire.

Ritual was observed in the byre, with the cattle being sained to protect them from disease and other ills.

At the end of the day it was satisfying if the household could review some pleasant hours spent in ensuring that good fortune would come in the ensuing twelvemonth — and in looking forward to another four seasons during which the lore-stock of the community could once again be brought into play to appease the unseen but ever-present spirit world.

Thus was time marked out in the Highland folk-year.

Its marking kept people in touch with the essential ingredients in their lives.

One wonders what our lives lack today, when, so often, we spend little enough time looking at out surroundings, our good fortunes, and all those small but important quiet times when we could reflect to some puropse.